FUDS

• A COMPLETE ENCYCLOFOODIA •

from **TICKLING SHRIMP** *to*

NOT DYING IN A RESTAURANT

By **ALFREDO & ANTONIO MIZRETTI,**

The

*Mizretti Brothers**

* Actually by **KELLY HUDSON**, **DAN KLEIN**, and **ARTHUR MEYER**

Illustrated by **NANCY JANUZZI**

BLOOMSBURY

NEW YORK · LONDON · NEW DELHI · SYDNEY

Published by Bloomsbury USA, New York

Bloomsbury is a trademark of Bloomsbury Publishing Plc

All papers used by Bloomsbury USA are natural, recyclable products made from wood grown in well-managed forests. The manufacturing processes conform to the environmental regulations of the country of origin.

Library of Congress Cataloging-in-Publication Data

Mizretti, Alfredo.
FUDS: a complete encylofoodia from tickling shrimp to not dying in a restaurant / by Alfredo and Antonio Mizretti, "The Mizretti Brothers" ; actually by Kelly Hudson, Dan Klein, and Arthur Meyer.—First U.S. edition.
pages cm
Includes bibliographical references and index.
ISBN 978-1-62040-314-3 (alk. paper)
1. Restaurants—Humor. 2. Cookbooks—Parodies, imitations, etc. 3. Cooking—Humor. 4. American wit and humor. I. Mizretti, Antonio. II. Hudson, Kelly. III. Klein, Dan (Comedian) IV. Meyer, Arthur (Comedian) V. Mizretti Brothers. VI. Title.
PN6231.R43M59 2014
818'.602—dc23
2014004775

First U.S. Edition 2015

1 3 5 7 9 10 8 6 4 2

Designed by Paul Kepple and Ralph Geroni at Headcase Design

Printed in China by Toppan Leefung Printing Ltd

Bloomsbury books may be purchased for business or promotional use. For information on bulk purchases please contact Macmillan Corporate and Premium Sales Department at specialmarkets@macmillan.com.

CONTENTS

Dedicated to Food.

BOOK APPETIZER

FOREWORD BY MARIO BATALI

LOOK, I'LL BE honest, I don't know why I'm writing this foreword. When the Mizretti Brothers first asked me to write this, I thought to myself, "Who are these men and why are they talking to me?"

WE CHATTED A little, I got to know them, and I discovered I did not like them. Their voices were too loud and their breath smelled like old coffee. So I'm not writing this because I like these guys or know them or think they practice good hygiene. And I am certainly not writing this because it's a good book. I read the book. It's not good. It's not a good book. You just bought a bad book. Have you looked at some of the dishes? They're disgusting. "Clumps of Turkey in a Bed of Heavy Tomato Scum with Softened Rice Poles"? "Dead Dog Co-Plated with Yam Clippings and a Leafy Sage Dumping"? "Chicken Francese That's Actually Just Rice"? Also, I'm pretty sure there's cocaine in one of their recipes. That's not cool, and it's very dangerous. Do not make that recipe.

I'M NOT WRITING this for the exposure, either. I'm Mario Fucking Batali. Shorts. Crocs. Little red ponytail. You know who the fuck I am. I don't need this stinky little book.

AM I DOING this because I love cookbooks? No. I hate cookbooks. I've put out like a dozen of my own, so I know the truth: cookbooks are ruining cooking. I make everything from scratch. Like a man! People who use cookbooks are cowards. If you love following directions so much, go build an end table from IKEA. Coward.

To be honest, I don't even like food that much. Sure, it's fun to make and it smells good. But, come on, it's just food.

HERE ARE FIVE THINGS I'D RATHER BE DOING RIGHT NOW THAN WRITING THIS:

1.

Learning to play the piano.

2.

Replacing my roof gutter.

3.

Writing a foreword to a much better book.

4.

Cutting my fingerprints off.

5.

Literally anything else.

So yeah, I don't know why I did this.

Mario Batali, New York, 2015

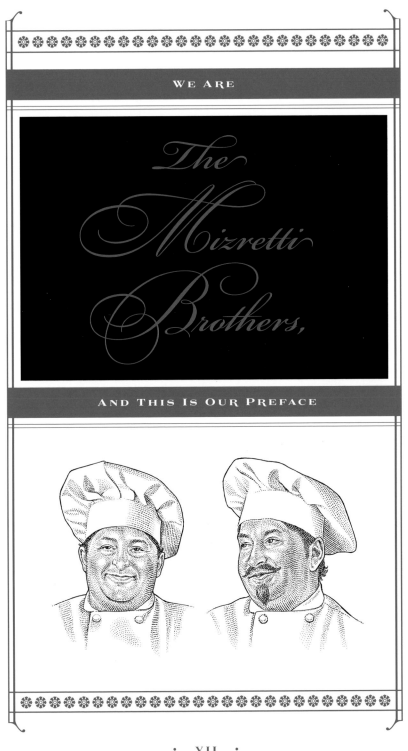

The *Mizretti Brothers,*

AND THIS IS OUR PREFACE

E MET EACH other when we were born. We are twin brothers who were born at the exact same moment. That's right, folks, it was a tie.

WE HAVE BEEN passionate about food since that very moment. Even on our first day on this earth, we ate food. And we began to notice a pattern: We would eat early in the day, then at a middle point in the day, and then later on we'd eat for a third time. And sometimes, we would eat for a fourth time, and that would often be something that tasted better because it had a lot of sugar in it. We knew then that we wanted to dedicate our lives to food. And sure enough, we haven't gone a single day without eating since the day we met.

"FOOD ISN'T JUST FOOD. FOOD IS MORE THAN FOOD." — *Us*

WHEN WE WERE growing up in our native city of Denver, Colorado, Mama Mizretti would cook us traditional homemade meals, like her Mama's Spaghetti and Meatballs, her Cranberry Bean Pasta Fagioli, and her special Vanilla Panna Cotta.

AND ALL OF it was awful. It tasted so bad. She must have used the shittiest ingredients. The stuff we ate was so bad that we smelled bad even after we showered. Mama Mizretti was a bad person and a bad cook, and the latter is what made us want to become chefs. Which we are today.

WE OPENED FUDS in Brooklyn in the mid-2000s as the borough was becoming the center of a burgeoning foodie revolution. We didn't know much then, and we had even less. In fact, FUDS's first menu had only three items: ketchup, bread, and milk.

MANY GREAT ARTISTS are influenced by their peers, and similarly, we were influenced by all the restaurants around us. There was one restaurant that had Thai food on their menu.

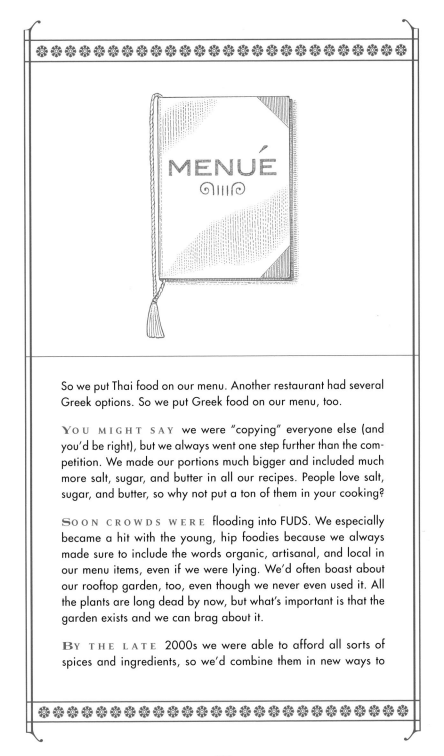

MENUÉ

So we put Thai food on our menu. Another restaurant had several Greek options. So we put Greek food on our menu, too.

YOU MIGHT SAY we were "copying" everyone else (and you'd be right), but we always went one step further than the competition. We made our portions much bigger and included much more salt, sugar, and butter in all our recipes. People love salt, sugar, and butter, so why not put a ton of them in your cooking?

SOON CROWDS WERE flooding into FUDS. We especially became a hit with the young, hip foodies because we always made sure to include the words organic, artisanal, and local in our menu items, even if we were lying. We'd often boast about our rooftop garden, too, even though we never even used it. All the plants are long dead by now, but what's important is that the garden exists and we can brag about it.

BY THE LATE 2000s we were able to afford all sorts of spices and ingredients, so we'd combine them in new ways to keep things interesting. You know how when you see something shiny, you want to look at it? Well that's exactly what we were doing, but with food. We had no idea what we were doing, but at least we looked smart.

SOME OF THE experimentation failed badly. Sure, several customers died from eating our cyanide-encrusted salmon and our bleach ravioli, but on the other hand, way more people became interested in our restaurant after hearing people died there. In the end, our failures and accidental murders only helped our reputation as one of the most unconventional and exciting restaurants in the city.

AND THEREIN LIES the success of FUDS. We are willing to do anything to be successful. We are fearless. We are not afraid to copy. We are not afraid to lie. We are not afraid to use lots and lots of butter.

MOST COOKBOOKS WOULD not include a recipe that tells you to go to Boston Market and order from their menu (see page 82). But we are unconventional. And that's why we're so rich and famous now, and that's what we'd like to pass on to you, the reader.

"FOOD ISN'T JUST FOOD. FOOD IS MORE THAN FOOD." — *Us*

AND EVEN AFTER ten years of running our own wildly successful restaurant, we remain passionate about all aspects of food. Food is the best. It's the best-tasting thing on earth. We have tried to eat other things that aren't food, like leather shoes and cameras, and none of it tastes as good as food.

WE HAD THOUSANDS of things to say about food, so that is why we have written this book. Writing a book was so fucking hard, though. You have to write so many words, and it's just so hard. After finally completing the book, we can both safely say that we are absolutely sick of each other and we want to spend way less time together. But it's hard to do that because we're married to twin sisters and we all live together, so we can't get away. We all sleep in the same big bed.

WE HOPE THAT you enjoy our insights and appreciate our recipes, and just remember . . .

"*Food isn't just food. Food is more than food.*"

—*Alfredo and Antonio Mizretti*

MEET
THE MIZRETTIS

MIZRETTI BROTHERS FACTS AND STATS

WHEN READING ABOUT food, it's important that you learn about the people who are writing about the food, also known as the "book authors." Please take a moment to learn about us (the "book authors").

ALFREDO MIZRETTI

HEIGHT: .... 5′ 2″

WEIGHT: .... Fat man

PREFERS: .... Baths to showers

NUMBER OF DOGS KILLED BECAUSE THEY "STARTLED" HIM: 16

FAVORITE FOOD: .... Velveeta Shells & Cheese

FAVORITE FOOD WORD: .... Zucchini

OPINION OF FUNNEL CAKE: .... That it's great

DAYS HE CAN GO WITHOUT MASTURBATING: 2

FEARS: .... Lions, weapons

FAVORITE STYLE OF SHIRT: .... Crew neck

FAVORITE MUSICAL GENRE: .... Reggae parody

NUMBER OF CUSTOMERS INTENTIONALLY POISONED: 64

NUMBER OF CUSTOMERS ACCIDENTALLY POISONED: 62

ANTONIO MIZRETTI

HEIGHT: .... 5′ 3″

WEIGHT: .... Fat man

NUMBER OF WOMEN RAVISHED IN FUDS KITCHEN FREEZER: 1

SANDPAPER ALLERGY: .... Yes

FAVORITE FOOD: .... Fruit skins

FAVORITE FOOD WORD: .... Whisk

FIRST KISS: .... Sophomore year of high school

FAVORITE WORKOUT: .... Jumping jacks

OPINION OF FUNNEL CAKE: .... That it's good, but not great

FAVORITE THING TO WEAR: .... "I'm a jeans-and-T-shirt kind of guy."

EYE COLOR: .... Not sure, gotta check

BEEN TO THE CIRCUS: .... Yes

MUSCLES PULLED IN THE KITCHEN: ...... Hamstring, quadriceps, butt

MIZRETTI BROTHERS'
AWARDS AND ACCOLADES

2011 Greasiest Grill Award

2004 Excellence in Saltiness Award

The Mona Ward Award for Outstanding Use of Tongs

2007 Best After Dinner Mints (4th Place)

2005 Placie Award for Best Place Mats

2nd Place at the 2010 Mizretti Family Chili Cook-off

2009 Nobel Prize for Pancakes

The Clean Chef Pants Award for Cleanest Chef Pants in
Brooklyn

Bronze Baster Award for Basting (Spring 2006)

2010 Certificate for Loudest Kitchen

2008 Tummy Award Nominee

The Leathery Food Award for Most Leather Used in Food

#19 on the *Huffington Post*'s "22 Fairly New Restaurants You
Should Consider Going To"

Honorary Degree from Miami Culinary Institute of Russia

2008 Academy Award for Best Sound Design

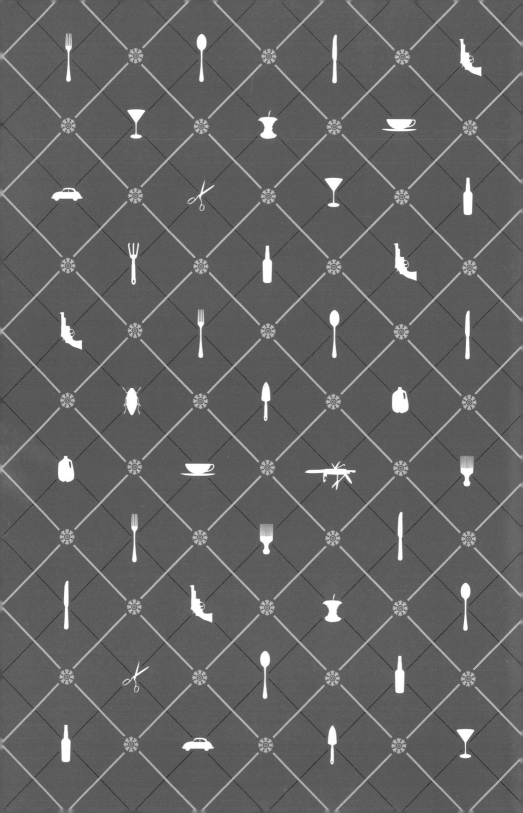

~ 1 ~

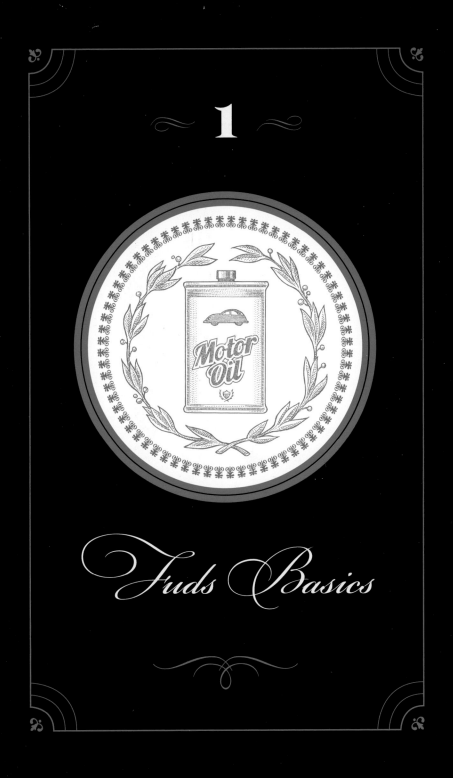

Fuds Basics

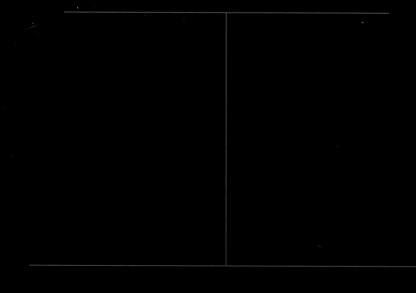

BEFORE YOU CAN SUCCESSFULLY digest food, your body must break it down to its simplest elements. The same can be said for understanding food. In this section, we'll answer all of your food-related questions, no matter how dumb they are.

WHAT IS FOOD?

WAIT. ARE YOU serious? "*What is food?*" Wow, I can't believe we have to try to answer that. It seems like if you're able to comprehend this sentence, you should know what food is. You were smart enough to buy this book, right? So how do you not know what food is?

Ugh, okay, it's hard to explain. It's like pizza and hamburgers and chicken—stuff like that. You know it when you see it. It's food. **FOOD IS FOOD.**

Okay? Moron . . .

F.O.O.D.

FEW PEOPLE KNOW that *food* is not actually a word, but an acronym—F.O.O.D.—invented by highly literate cavemen.

- **F**UNCTIONAL

- **O**RGANIC

- **O**RGANISM

- **D**IET

So if you ever forget the word *food*, just step outside, remember its root acronym, finish your cigarette, and hop right back into that conversation you were having about food.

"MAY I ONE DAY BE REMEMBERED FOR MY SWISS OMELETS."

—*Marie Curie,* PHYSICIST AND CHEMIST

FOOD QAAS

PEOPLE FREQUENTLY ASK us questions about food, which is why we thought it'd be helpful to include some QAAs—Questions Asked A Lot.

WHERE DOES FOOD COME FROM?

Stores.

IS FOOD GOOD?

For the most part, yes, food is very good. But different people like different foods. For instance, we fucking hate black olives, but we know some dipshits who like them.

WHY DOES FOOD GET THROWN AWAY?

That's not food, that's trash. Trash and food are two different things.

WHAT IS THE BEST FOOD?

Eggs Benedict wrapped in gold.

HOW MUCH FOOD IS THERE?

So much.

IS THERE ENOUGH FOOD FOR EVERYONE?

What do you mean?

AM I FOOD?

Yep. Sorry.

WHEN CAN YOU GET FOOD?

Food is put on sale at eight a.m.

WHO HAS THE MOST FOOD?

The king.

WHAT IS THE MOST FOOD SOMEONE CAN HAVE?

A whole turkey with mashed potatoes and stuffing.

HOW MUCH DOES FOOD COST?

Like five to ten bucks.

IS IT OKAY TO FILL UP ON BREAD?

Yes. And not only is it okay, but we encourage it! The funniest situation would be if you ordered your meal, then filled up on bread, and then by the time your meal came, you would say to the waiter, "I'm sorry, I filled up on bread. I'm not hungry anymore." Try that the next time you go out.

WHAT SHOULD YOU SAY WHEN YOU WANT FOOD?

"Please give me food" or "Give that to me now."

WHAT HAPPENS WHEN YOU COMBINE EVERY SINGLE FOOD INTO ONE?

You get a turkey sandwich with Swiss cheese, mayo, and honey mustard on ciabatta bread.

IS A BANANA FOOD?

No. A banana has a peel on it, and no one eats the peel, so a banana is not food. We have never tried unpeeling a banana, it's too risky. We don't know what could be under there.

IS FOOD ART?

It depends. If you go to a bowing alley and see some cheese fries on a table, it is not art. However, if you see those same cheese fries in a glass case at an art museum, it's part of an exhibit, so it is art.

WHAT WILL WE EAT IN THE FUTURE?

Food.

WHY IS SOME FOOD WET AND SOME FOOD DRY?

At this point, you're asking too many questions. Let's just move on.

"KNOWLEDGE IS POWER. MY LAST NAME IS BACON."

—Francis Bacon, PHILOSOPHER

HOW TO EAT

IF YOU'RE GOING TO GET THE MOST OUT of this cookbook, you must know how to eat.

Eating is one of the best ways to enjoy food. But did you know that you're probably doing it wrong? Most people rush through their meals, wolfing down large chunks of beef like they was fat. Believe it or not, there actually is a right way to eat, which, when done successfully, will ensure full enjoyment of your meal.

1.

Sit down in your chair and tuck yourself up to the table's edge so that it is firmly pressed against your stomach. Make sure your knees are bent at a 90-degree angle and that your enshoed feet are planted flat against the floor.

2.

Breathe in deeply and hold your breath. DO NOT EXHALE.

3.

Bring your hand from beneath the table to above it. Slowly contour all five fingers around your fork as if grasping the skinny neck of a sleeping enemy.

4.

With the prongs of your fork, lightly poke your food to see what happens. Then spear your food, making sure the fork steadily penetrates your food's body.

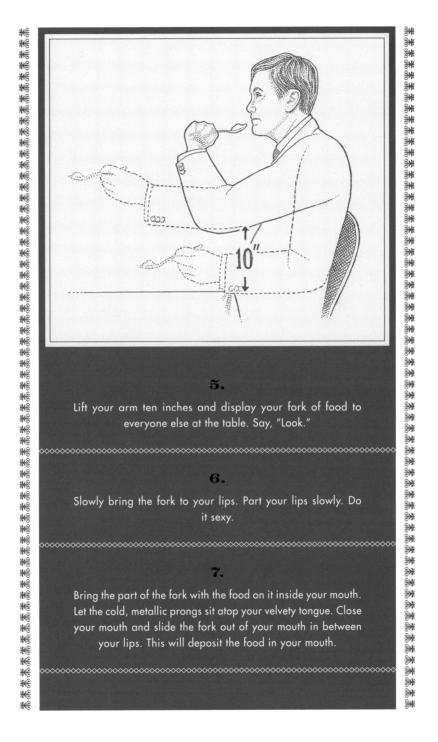

5.

Lift your arm ten inches and display your fork of food to everyone else at the table. Say, "Look."

6.

Slowly bring the fork to your lips. Part your lips slowly. Do it sexy.

7.

Bring the part of the fork with the food on it inside your mouth. Let the cold, metallic prongs sit atop your velvety tongue. Close your mouth and slide the fork out of your mouth in between your lips. This will deposit the food in your mouth.

8.

Using your teeth, grind the food up, down, and all around.
It may seem mean to do this, but remember, we're humans.
We won.

9.

Continue letting the food tumble about the inside of your mouth.
Use your tongue to notice the texture and temperature of your
food. Jot that information down in your FUDS Handbook.

10.

Using your esophagus (or maybe it's your lungs), swallow the
food down your throat. This part is somewhat sad because it
means saying good-bye to the bite of food that you just met.
But don't worry. It'll still be in your body for a few more hours
before you shit it out. Heh heh heh.

11.

EXHALE.

Repeat this process for every bite of food you take. A typical
meal should take three and a half hours.

TONGUE DIAGRAM

This is a map of the human tongue. It is divided into many sections, each of which corresponds to a different taste, as shown here.

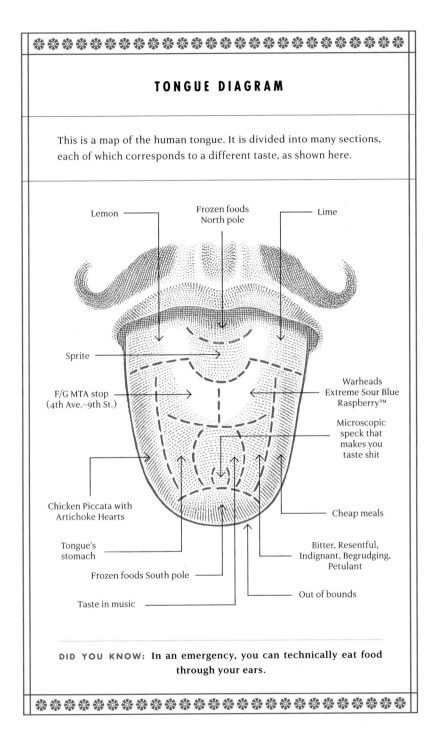

Lemon

Frozen foods North pole

Lime

Sprite

F/G MTA stop (4th Ave.–9th St.)

Warheads Extreme Sour Blue Raspberry™

Microscopic speck that makes you taste shit

Chicken Piccata with Artichoke Hearts

Cheap meals

Tongue's stomach

Bitter, Resentful, Indignant, Begrudging, Petulant

Frozen foods South pole

Taste in music

Out of bounds

DID YOU KNOW: In an emergency, you can technically eat food through your ears.

TIME AND FOOD:
A FOOD TIMELINE

CONTRARY TO POPULAR belief, food has been around for more than just the last one hundred years. And in order to better understand food now, it is important to learn what food has gone through, and the hardships it has faced. We have prepared a timeline to teach you about the most important moments in the history of food.

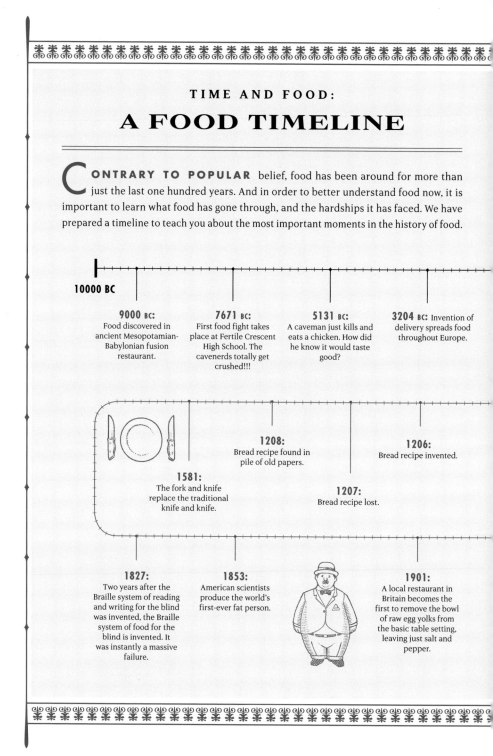

10000 BC

9000 BC:
Food discovered in ancient Mesopotamian-Babylonian fusion restaurant.

7671 BC:
First food fight takes place at Fertile Crescent High School. The cavenerds totally get crushed!!!

5131 BC:
A caveman just kills and eats a chicken. How did he know it would taste good?

3204 BC: Invention of delivery spreads food throughout Europe.

1208:
Bread recipe found in pile of old papers.

1206:
Bread recipe invented.

1581:
The fork and knife replace the traditional knife and knife.

1207:
Bread recipe lost.

1827:
Two years after the Braille system of reading and writing for the blind was invented, the Braille system of food for the blind is invented. It was instantly a massive failure.

1853:
American scientists produce the world's first-ever fat person.

1901:
A local restaurant in Britain becomes the first to remove the bowl of raw egg yolks from the basic table setting, leaving just salt and pepper.

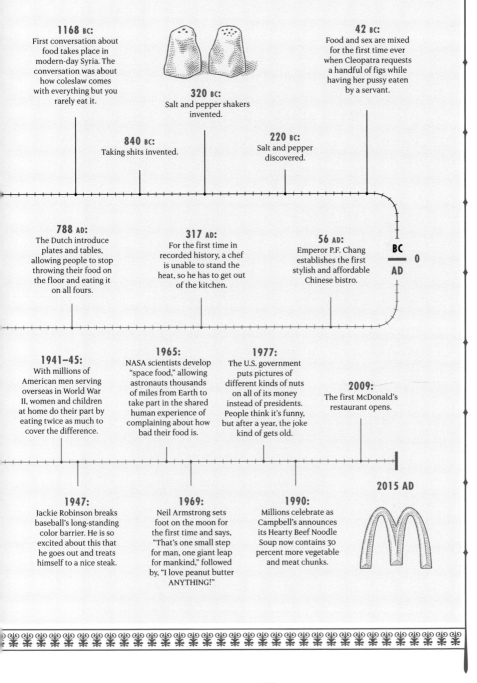

1168 BC:
First conversation about food takes place in modern-day Syria. The conversation was about how coleslaw comes with everything but you rarely eat it.

320 BC:
Salt and pepper shakers invented.

42 BC:
Food and sex are mixed for the first time ever when Cleopatra requests a handful of figs while having her pussy eaten by a servant.

840 BC:
Taking shits invented.

220 BC:
Salt and pepper discovered.

788 AD:
The Dutch introduce plates and tables, allowing people to stop throwing their food on the floor and eating it on all fours.

317 AD:
For the first time in recorded history, a chef is unable to stand the heat, so he has to get out of the kitchen.

56 AD:
Emperor P.F. Chang establishes the first stylish and affordable Chinese bistro.

BC
0
AD

1941–45:
With millions of American men serving overseas in World War II, women and children at home do their part by eating twice as much to cover the difference.

1965:
NASA scientists develop "space food," allowing astronauts thousands of miles from Earth to take part in the shared human experience of complaining about how bad their food is.

1977:
The U.S. government puts pictures of different kinds of nuts on all of its money instead of presidents. People think it's funny, but after a year, the joke kind of gets old.

2009:
The first McDonald's restaurant opens.

1947:
Jackie Robinson breaks baseball's long-standing color barrier. He is so excited about this that he goes out and treats himself to a nice steak.

1969:
Neil Armstrong sets foot on the moon for the first time and says, "That's one small step for man, one giant leap for mankind," followed by, "I love peanut butter ANYTHING!"

1990:
Millions celebrate as Campbell's announces its Hearty Beef Noodle Soup now contains 30 percent more vegetable and meat chunks.

2015 AD

THINGS YOU SHOULD NEVER EAT

1. Cars

2. Friends and other people

3. Wet cement, even though it may look like a delicious gray milkshake

4. Some carpet

5. Field goalposts

6. Corn

7. 1980s stereo equipment

8. Weapons

9. Trees

10. Wedding dresses

11. Books (but this book is actually edible)

12. Cone-shaped objects and all other objects

13. Dog shit

14. Stone tablets with the Ten Commandments on them

15. Delicious-looking doctor's equipment like stethoscopes

16. Boxes

17. Ghosts (impossible to eat anyway, but we had to put this here/we wanted to remind you)

Chef's Nook

EDWARD THE BLOND: After being named Best Chef of 1219 by *Time Out Essex*, Edward allowed the praise to go to his head and became known as the First Asshole Chef. Today, many chefs honor Edward by acting like pompous, self-obsessed assholes.

DID YOU KNOW: From the years 1524 to 1527, there was no food anywhere.

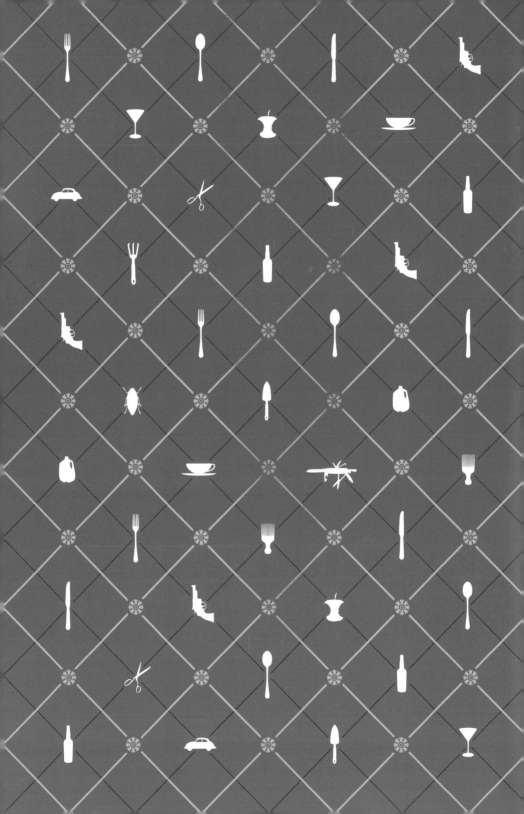

~2~

Kitchen

THE KITCHEN. THIS IS WHERE ALL the food stuff goes down. Hey, kitchen sounds a lot like chicken, doesn't it? Think that's a co-incidence? Well, maybe in this section you'll find out why* . . .

* We are legally obligated to tell you that you will not find out why.

KITCHEN THINGS

A **LOT OF PEOPLE** think that cooking is just throwing a bunch of ingredients together and getting them all hot. That's true, but there are plenty of tools that can help ease the process. Here are a few of our favorites. We recommend you spend a lot of money on them.

AIR, SURFACES, AND SPACE

The three most important things you'll need in your kitchen are breathable air, matter in the shape of surfaces, and spatial dimensions. Without air, you cannot breathe; without surfaces, you have no place to put the food; and without dimensions, you would be floating in an endless white void, and that's no good for cooking.

HANDS

Hands are the two things that hang off the ends of your arms. They're great for grabbing, holding, throwing, placing, and tickling your food. You get them for free when you are born. They're easy to maintain, too. Just remember to wash them at least once a week.

SPANKLER
For spanking food when it's cooking too loudly in the pan.

CLOSED SPOON
The only spoon that has no opening so nothing can get inside or out.
Great for cooking.

SMALL COOKING ROCK
For smashing hard-to-open things, like cans and bottles.

LARGE COOKING ROCK
For smashing larger hard-to-open things, like big cans and windows.

BROADSWORD
For chopping large hunks of meat and defending your kitchen against
invading infantrymen.

TARP
Cover your entire kitchen with a thick blue plastic tarp so when you're
finished cooking, you can remove it and *Voilà!* No mess. This is much
more convenient than tearing down and rebuilding your kitchen from
scratch every time you make a mess.

NAILS AND SCREWS
These will come in handy when you need ingredients to stick together.
Nails and screws, man.

REGULATION NCAA FOOTBALL
For having fun with.

BASEBALL BAT

Helps clear away dirty dishes, pots, and pans in one swing. Either toss them up in the air or simply hit them directly off the surface.

CEILING FOOD SWING

A swing connected to the ceiling that rocks your food back and forth to put it in a good mood before it's cooked.

VENDING MACHINE

Vending machines are great for when you don't want to cook food, and instead want to just buy candy and eat it.

SANDWICH SEPARATOR

For when two pieces of bread and some ingredients accidentally get stuck together in what's known as a "sandwich." This loud, refrigerator-size, gasoline-powered tool will tear them apart so you can eat them in the way they were intended to be eaten.

LARGE BOWL

For spitting in.

HOT LAVA

Add danger and excitement to your cooking experience by pouring ten gallons of hot lava in your kitchen. If you fall in it, you die.

FOOD MARBLES

A series of marbles used for cooking.

APRON

A protective garment worn over one's body. You don't need to wear anything underneath it. It's fine, you'll be okay.

FOOD DRESSES
For more formal cooking occasions.

PROTRACTOR
A semicircular tool for measuring angles.

UNIVERSAL WORMHOLE
Helps get rid of food scraps. Place them into the wormhole and send them to a far-off corner of the universe.

ROLLING PIN
Used to bop or bonk people on the head when they try to steal cooling pies off your windowsill. Otherwise useless.

TIMER
We like to set our timers for 1 minute. Even though the food isn't ready, it's a lot faster than what recipes tell you to set it for.

MORPHINE
Cooking can be stressful, so use a little morphine to calm down, pass out, and snooze through the cooking process.

SMALL, SPOON-SHAPED WALKING STICK
To get you from one side of the counter to the other.

WAFFLE IRON
This would have been a great weapon for them to have used in one of the *Home Alone* movies. We can't believe they didn't think of that.

"WHO KNOWS WHAT THE FUTURE HOLDS?
MAYBE SOME SORT OF COMPUTERIZED FOOD
OR SOMETHING?"

—*Bill Gates,* FOUNDER OF MICROSOFT

KNIVES

ONE WORD: KNIVES. Knives, man. Give it up for knives! KNIVES, KNIVES, KNIVES, KNIVES!! No question about it, knives are way cooler than forks or spoons will ever be. Have you ever heard of a Swiss Army Fork? No. Has anyone ever been stabbed in the kidney with a spoon? No. (We Googled it, and all we found was that one time a dog swallowed a plastic spoon, but he was rescued.) Here is a description of every type of knife you should have in your kitchen.

BLADELESS HANDLE
Great for pretending to chop something to make it look like you're too busy to help out around the house with other chores.

SOUP KNIFE
Knife used to cut soup.

PERFECT CIRCLE KNIFE
One perfect, circular blade that is impossible to use and extremely expensive.

THE FENCING FOIL
To poke and taunt your food before cooking.

KNIFE IN A ROCK
This knife can be used only by one pure of heart.

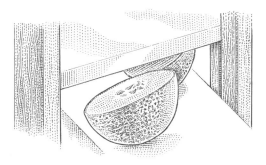

GUILLOTINE

Set an example by executing rotten food in front of the rest of the food.

OLD DULL KNIFE

We're not sure why we still have it. It may have belonged to one of our ex-girlfriends but it's in our kitchen, so we have to put it in the book.

AMARILLO EIGHTEEN-INCH BULL WHIP

Used to whip food in half. We strongly recommend a knife instead of a whip.

POKEY

A kid's steak knife that comes in various fun colors.

BOW AND ARROW

When you want to shoot your steak with arrows instead of cutting it with a knife.

"ON THE COUNT OF THREE, LET'S SAY WHAT
WE'RE IN THE MOOD FOR EATING RIGHT NOW: ONE . . .
TWO . . . THREE . . . BUFFALO! OH MY GOD,
WE BOTH SAID IT AT THE SAME TIME!
THAT'S SO WEIRD!"

— *Lewis and Clark,* EXPLORERS

PANTRY

THE PANTRY IS where you find all the stuff you would normally find in the pantry. Here's what's in our pantry.

HARD-STINK COOKING SOIL

A nice fourteen-pound bag of cooking soil bought fresh from an old man. Gives everything that rich, mildewy, straight-out-of-the-ground stink.

PIGEON OIL

Squeezed from a live pigeon, this oil gives sautéed dishes a delicious gamey and nutty taste. It's also just a great excuse to squeeze a pigeon.

TANNENBAUM'S CANNED GUN POWDER

Gives food that extra bang because it's explosive and inedible.

CANNED SEA DIRT IN FISHWATER

Great for giving foods that just-washed-up-on-the-shore-of-Coney-Island taste that we all crave.

GLASS SPRINKLETTES

Add texture as well as a sharp, dangerous pain to any dessert.

JAR OF OLD POOL PENNIES

Top off a hot meal with some old pool pennies for luck and a nice copper finish. Dinner guests won't mind spitting them up as long as they get a good wish out of it.

#2 PENCIL SHAVINGS

Give meals that natural woody, leady, and chubby-finger flavor. For best results, we recommend foraging for them in their natural environment: an elementary school Dumpster.

FRUIT GARBAGE PIECES

The stems and rinds are terrible to eat on the fruit, but they will help your guests appreciate how good your cooking would have been had it not been covered in dirty, disgusting food garbage.

CINNAMON TOAST CRUNCH

You don't need this for any recipes, but there are several times in the day when you'll be thinking, I could really go for a handful of Cinnamon Toast Crunch right now, and then it will be there and you can eat it.

ROADSIDE WINTER SALT

You know those huge pyramid-shaped storage units where they keep the salt for snowstorms? Sneak in there with a large sack and take some for free.

FULLY GROWN MAPLE TREE

Planting a fifty-foot tree in your pantry will require major construction and upkeep (raccoons, peckers, etc.), and you'll be stuck with about twenty-five large barrels of syrup every year. Having a fully grown maple tree in your house is not good.

WHAT'S IN OUR SPICE RACK

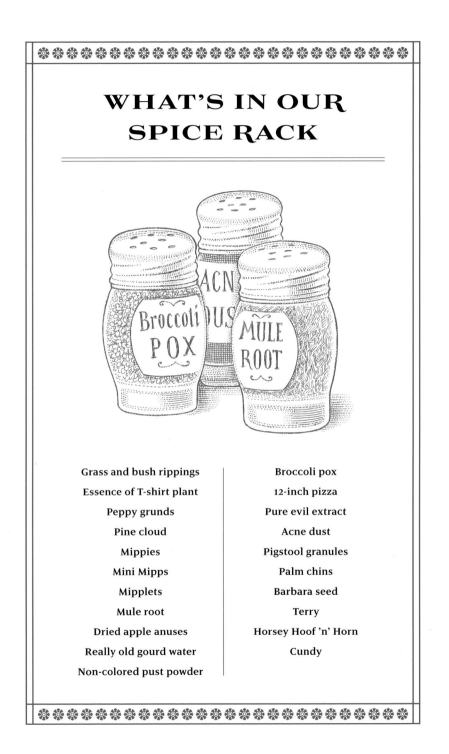

Grass and bush rippings

Essence of T-shirt plant

Peppy grunds

Pine cloud

Mippies

Mini Mipps

Mipplets

Mule root

Dried apple anuses

Really old gourd water

Non-colored pust powder

Broccoli pox

12-inch pizza

Pure evil extract

Acne dust

Pigstool granules

Palm chins

Barbara seed

Terry

Horsey Hoof 'n' Horn

Cundy

SAFETY IN THE KITCHEN

SAFETY IN THE KITCHEN SHOULD *ALWAYS* be the chef's number-six priority, next to having fun (number one), making food (two), making noises with pots and pans (three), stinking up the house (four), and breaking a good, thick sweat (five).

The key to safety in the kitchen is patience and gracefulness. At the very least, clumsy chefs will often lose a finger during a vigorous cooking sesh. They could die, too. At any moment, anyone could die. Here are some tips to avoid death in the kitchen (you're on your own in other places).

Always pad your body and hands with old pillows.

Wash hands in a large bucket of standing water with the other members of the kitchen staff. The good germs from everyone's hands will neutralize the bad germs.

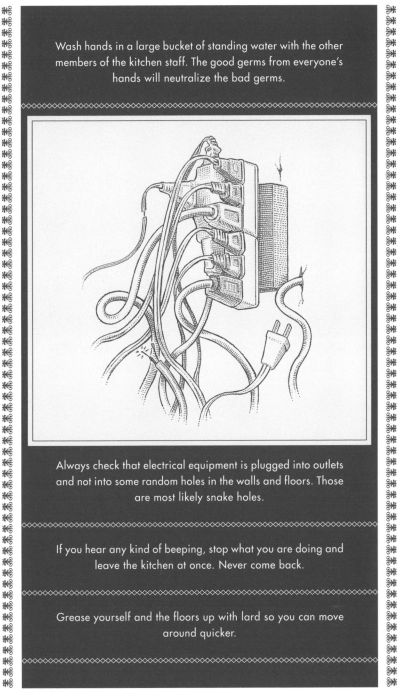

Always check that electrical equipment is plugged into outlets and not into some random holes in the walls and floors. Those are most likely snake holes.

If you hear any kind of beeping, stop what you are doing and leave the kitchen at once. Never come back.

Grease yourself and the floors up with lard so you can move around quicker.

If someone in the kitchen is holding a knife, take it away from them and stab them first. Remember: in the kitchen it's you versus everyone.

Never let children into a kitchen. They may have a gun.

If you have to cough or sneeze, do it on the food. You don't want to get any germs on your hands.

To avoid a fire, hose down all electrical outlets and equipment. Get them good and wet, because water puts out fire.

Wear tight, sexy clothing in the kitchen at all times. Firemen always save the sexiest people first.

Turn off the lights while you are cooking so you don't forget to turn them off later.

No socks or shoes in the kitchen!

Cook as fast and as hard as you can to leave less time for something to go wrong.

Watch out! There's something right behind you! Actually, there's not, but you gotta have that attitude about this stuff.

DID YOU KNOW: In 1991, a truck carrying Tostitos chips crashed into a truck carrying Chi-Chi's salsa. Three people were killed.

PROPER TABLE SETTING

OUR GREAT-GRANDBROTHER RAPHAELI was always sharing his wisdom with us. In fact, he was the one who told us to start wetting our toilet paper before wiping. And we've never gone back to the dry stuff since!

When he was on his deathbed, he left this world with one last bit of wisdom. He wanted to tell us how important proper table setting was. His words were as follows:

> [Imagine this all said in Raphaeli's thick Italian accent. He also had a speech impediment where he couldn't say *s*'s, so keep that in mind too.] One simply cannot overstate the importance of a proper table setting. [Imagine this part more angrily.] In fact, an improper placement of wares is a virulent insult to any meal and to the chef who prepared said meal. Neither I nor any member of the House of Chesterton shall stand for the lowly manners of a common gutter rat! [We aren't sure where Raphaeli came up with the House of Chesterton, but he was about to die, so we didn't question him!] Thusly, if I EVER [Raphaeli's final heart attack started here.] *acckkkkuggghhh* [Whispered] Wait! Before I die, before I breathe my last breath, please, go to the attic. The key to the family locket is in—[Raphaeli died.]

So we never found out where in the attic the key to the family locket is. In fact, none of us cares to find it. Who cares about lockets! Here is a proper dinner-table setting:

1. SPOON PEDESTAL

2. GLASS-TAPPING SPOON—for getting the room's attention or forcing two people to kiss even if they don't want to

3. SECRET FORK—a fork taped to the bottom of the table

4. DESSERT SCISSORS

5. PENCIL and PAPER for dinner notes

6. SOUP STOOL and SALAD BENCH

7. SECURITY-CHECKPOINT BOWL—for storing your keys, watch, loose change, and boarding pass during a meal

8. NAPKIN POLE—attached like a flag and pulled to full mast at the beginning of the meal

9. END ZONE—if guest's food crosses into this section of the table, he receives six points

10. RUSTY CROWBAR

11. REVENGE KNIFE—to stab the person sitting to your left

12. FINGER FIRE—a little campfire for warming your fingers

13. NINE-PLATE STACK—a stack of nine plates

14. TABLE DICK—covered by the tablecloth

15. CLEAR GLASS CYLINDER—don't put anything in it

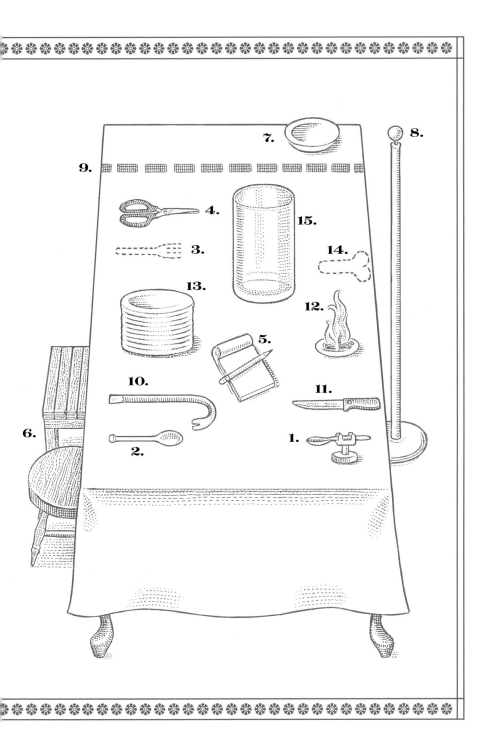

MEASUREMENT CONVERSIONS

MEASUREMENTS*

1 cup = 1 cup	2 gallons = 2 breasts	8 cups = 1 buttload
$^{11}/_{12}$ cup = 1 stupid cup	2 quarts = 1 Jeffrey	2 buttloads = 1 pantload
$^1/_9$ cup = 1 prince's pinky	4 quarts = 1 Big Jeffrey	4 pantloads = 1 shitload
$^3/_{19}$ cup = hard to measure	$^1/_2$ quart = 1 Young Jeff	10 shitloads = 1 shit-ton
1,000 cups = 1 big-ass bucket	1 pint = $^1/_2$ double pint	
	8 fluid ounces = 1 big piss	1 Ryan Gosling = 177 pounds
1 teaspoon = 4 belly buttons	10 toddler handfuls = 1 lumberjack's handful	

COOKING TIMES

5/8 minute = 37.5 seconds	15 minutes = 1 teenage masturbation session	1 bad minute = 60 seconds that suck
1 fisherman's minute = 2 minutes	3 hours = 1 *Braveheart*	1 horse day = time it takes to eat a horse

* We will not use any of these measurement or time conversions in this book.

"MY GREATEST REGRET
IS NEVER HAVING TRIED
AN OLIVE."

—*Ernest Hemingway*, AUTHOR

TALLEST CHEF: Standing at six foot eight, Frenchman Adrien Fournier was the tallest chef in recorded history. Though he was able to "see more in the kitchen," Fournier lacked an interest in food preparation and was fired from his post two days after being hired, when he was discovered forcing a live owl inside a pumpkin. Fournier is still widely blamed for the common stereotype that tall people are bad at everything.

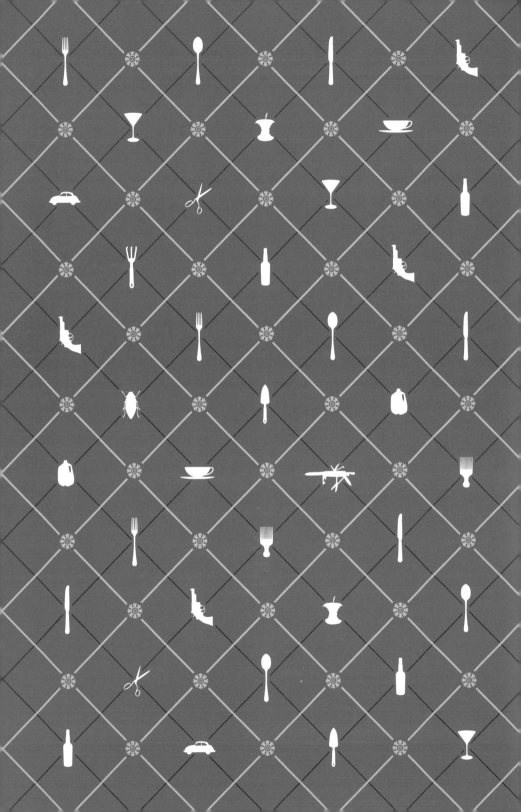

~3~

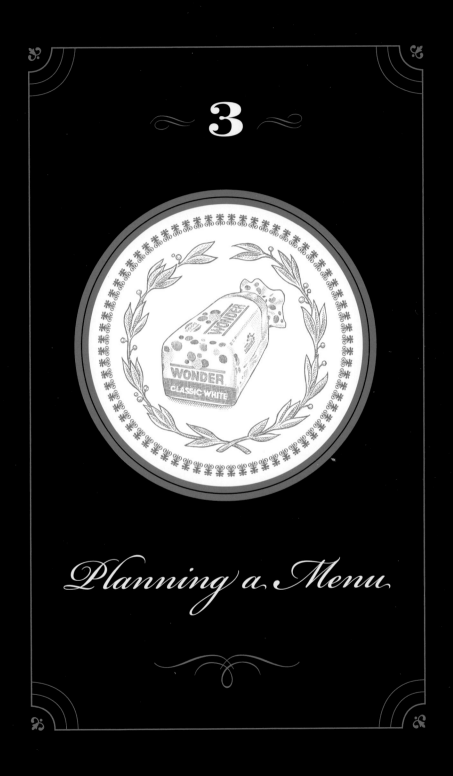

Planning a Menu

EVERY DAY, PEOPLE ASK US WHY our menu looks so good. The short answer is we paid a guy named Edmond to design it for us. The long answer is that it took years of cultivating and planning. When deciding which items to include in your restaurant, many things need to be taken into consideration: Is this food good? Is it cheap? There are some other questions too. The following sections will help you better understand food, especially if you are hoping to make your own menu one day.*

* Please don't open your own restaurant, as it may compete with ours and take away our business.

TYPES OF FOOD

FOR A COMPLETE balanced meal, it is optimal for your dishes to contain different kinds of foods (not just a whole bunch of spaghetti). The most common types of food are hot, cold, good, and bad. We like to incorporate one of each, and when planning your own menu, you should too.*

Once again, please do not open a competing restaurant. We already have enough problems.

HOT FOOD: Food that is smoking or sizzling when it is served, eliciting "oooh" and "aaah" sounds from nearby restaurant guests.

COLD FOOD: Food that you didn't heat up in the microwave because you are too lazy.

NATURAL FOOD: As disgusting as it sounds, natural food grows straight out of the ground. It's covered in dirt and sometimes there's bugs on it. Gross, right?

FAST FOOD: The best kind of food, fast food is made quickly, costs next to nothing, and smells great. Some people do not like fast food because they are jealous of how popular it is.

SLOW FOOD: Slow food is fast food that takes a really long time to come out. Slow food happens when it's really busy at Wendy's or the fryer is broken at Carl's Jr. and you have to wait. Sometimes they make you come back the next day.

GOOD FOOD: Any food that tastes good because it has a lot of bacon, cheese, sugar, or ranch dressing on it. So basically a bacon ranch cheeseburger served on a donut.

BAD FOOD: See Natural Food.

SAD FOOD: Food you eat when you are sad, also known as a Tub of Ice Cream and Some Cinnamon Buns. This food makes you feel better by making you fatter. Your brain converts fat into happiness through the use of chemicals and stuff.

TRASH FOOD: Food that has been thrown into the trash. Depending on how long it's been in the trash, it may still be edible. Remember that *Seinfeld* episode where George eats an eclair out of the trash? Kramer also pees out his kidney stone at the circus in that episode.

DRY FOOD: Food that is not dripping wet with barbecue sauce, nacho cheese, or mayonnaise. Also known as "worthless food."

WET FOOD: Drinks.

DID YOU KNOW: When getting a fountain soda at a fast-food restaurant, it is always best to fill your drink to the tippy top.

NASTY PARTY
PLATTER

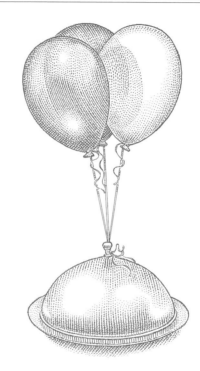

HAVING A PARTY is a great way to show off your ability to en-
tertain a group of people whom you have gathered together so that
they are forced to pay attention to you. And what better way to keep them
in your house than to provide them with lots of nasty snacks? Whether it's
dips, fingering foods, crasps, or little balls, the party snack is different from
your average food in that it requires you to use either your fingers or a small
stick of wood. Here is an average spread at the Mizretti household. Lick your
fingers and the palms of your hands, you're in for some treats!

TEN ESSENTIAL DIPS AND DRIPPINGS

1. Prune Melt
2. Wood Floor
3. Dirt Digger's Dip
4. Pea
5. Terry Pudding
6. Spice Mess
7. Ham Strength
8. Creamed Tan
9. Spinach Waters
10. Oak Oil with Drowned Peppercorns

PLATTER

Super Beef Ham Loaf

Chafing Meat Stones

Ham Girl Pin-Ups

Magic Rice Cob

Sugar Kisses on a Winter Boy's Nose

Carrot-Flavored Pool Pennies

Cooled Hot Flambo

Dancing Fruit Bobbies

Maxines

Cheesepretz Maxines

PARTY WETS

Pep-Cock Nog

Grode Cream Froth

Tropical Fruit Bath

DID YOU KNOW: There were eleven food-based sitcom pilots produced in 1989, including *Restaurant Family* and *What's Cookin'?*, but none of them went to series.

REGIONAL DISHES

PEOPLE'S TASTES VARY by region and, at FUDS, we pride ourselves on knowing all the different types of cuisines from all over the country. In fact, all restaurateurs must feature regional dishes in their selections, so when travelers walk past their restaurants, they have no excuse for not coming in. They're going to like something, and they'd better sit their bottom cheeks down and eat it. Below is a list of the country's most beloved dishes, by region.

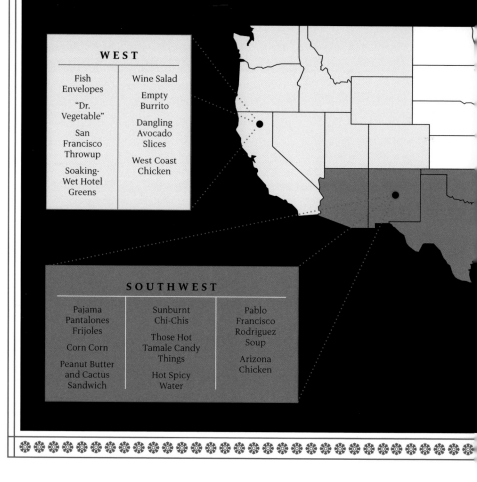

WEST

Fish Envelopes	Wine Salad
"Dr. Vegetable"	Empty Burrito
San Francisco Throwup	Dangling Avocado Slices
Soaking-Wet Hotel Greens	West Coast Chicken

SOUTHWEST

Pajama Pantalones Frijoles	Sunburnt Chi-Chis	Pablo Francisco Rodriguez Soup
Corn Corn	Those Hot Tamale Candy Things	Arizona Chicken
Peanut Butter and Cactus Sandwich	Hot Spicy Water	

MIDWEST

Chicago-Style Animal Insides

Plain Raw Corn

Schnitziewurst in a Bacon Bikini

Corn-Coated Corn-Stuffed Anything

Cheesy Dough Bowl

Heated Meat on a Paper Plate

Kansas City, Missouri, Chickens

NORTHEAST

Creamed Trout with a Pilgrim's Belt Buckle

New England Mayonnaise Toast

Chunky Barnacle Broth

New York Peetzer

Old People Slop

Dry Boston Brown Beans in Paper Sauce

Maine Chicken

DEEP SOUTH

Nushy Nushies

White Bread with Whiskey Dumped on It

Sugar Butter Pie with Sugar Butter Crust

Sprizzled Popkarn Okra

Great Grandma's Dead Little Horse

Carolina-Style Sauce-Covered Pig Arms

So Deeply Fried Snapping Turtle Knees

An Alligator Wearing Sunglasses

Softcover *Pelican Brief* with Gravy

Swollen Horndog

Louisiana Chicken

FOODS AND THEIR BABIES

WHEN TWO FOODS love each other, they form a special bond and have sex with each other. This results in a baby. No one has actually ever seen where and how food has sex, but we've definitely seen baby carrots, so it must be true. When running a restaurant, it's important to know whether you want an adult or a baby version of a food in a meal.* Here are some different foods and their babies. Aren't they cute?

* Not sure if this has set in yet, but just stop fantasizing about your own damn restaurant. It's sort of ridiculous that you'd buy this book and then stab us in the back by starting your own place. We need this restaurant more than you do. Cut it out.

Carrot—Baby carrot

Corn—Baby corn

Swiss cheese—Baby Swiss cheese

Hot dog—Cocktail weenie

Hamburger—Slider

Cake—Cupcake

Bagel—Mini-bagel

Donuts—Hostess Donettes

Jumbo shrimp— Popcorn shrimp

Large bucket of popcorn—Small bag of popcorn

Steak—Piece of steak

King-size Snickers— Fun-size Snickers

Food—Baby food

Back ribs—Baby back ribs

Slim Jim—Baby meat stick

Bread—Crumbs

Squash—(cannot reproduce)

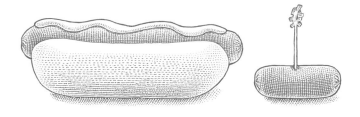

DID YOU KNOW: Most women like to be looked at while eating.

Chef's Nook

WILLIAM SHAKESPEARE: Widely referred to as the Loser of All Chefs, William Shakespeare was one of the most notorious failures of the 1500s. After he was invited to cook for the king and queen and subsequently mocked for his grotesque ham and biscuits, Shakespeare hurled his apron at a knight and claimed he would show the world his true talents, then ran off sobbing. No one heard from him ever again.

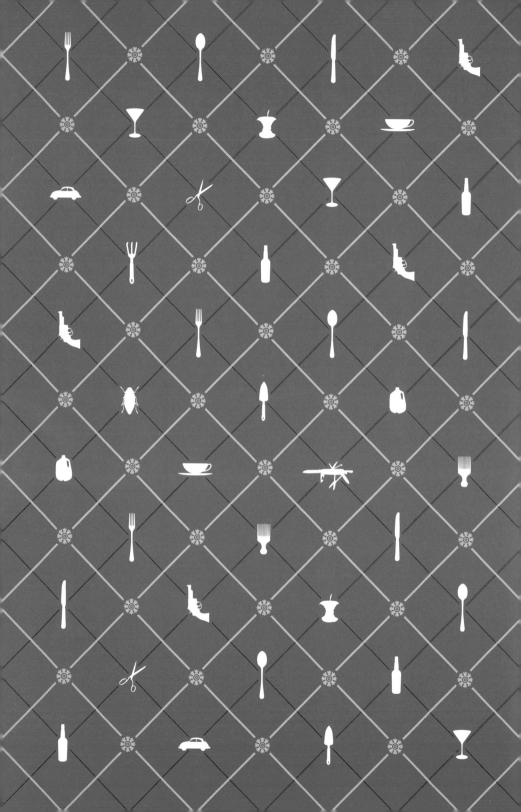

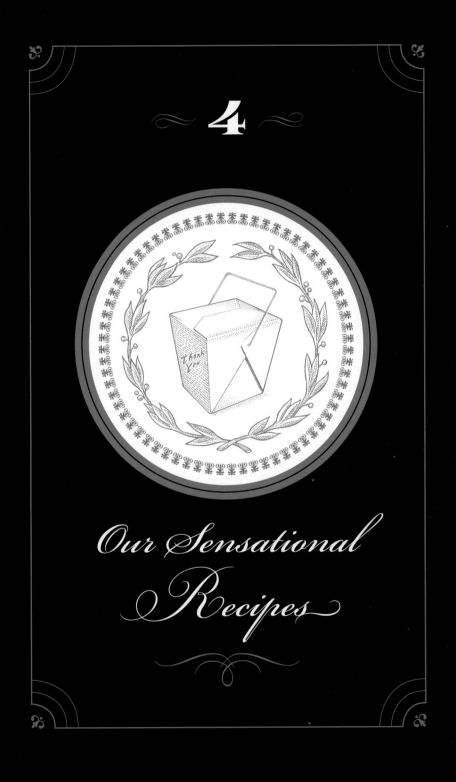

4

Our Sensational Recipes

SO YOU'VE LEARNED ALL YOU CAN *about food. Now it's time to turn that food into food. No, don't just start smashing ingredients together as hard as you can. Instead, follow these recipes to create some of your favorite FUDS concoctions from the comfort of your own sad, dirty, small apartment.*

MEAL
BEGINNINGS

MEAL BEGINNINGS PRAYER

Meal Beginnings, you give us confidence and hope. Hope that we may conquer our entire meal, for you are so inconsequential and puny. So small, so weak, so oniony, so battered and fried, so perfect for eating while watching the Super Bowl. Lift us from our hunger, O Meal Beginnings, and deliver us to our steak. **AMEN.**

Mixed Chilled-and-Heated Ploppers

Most dishes are hot or cold. This one is hot and cold. That doesn't mean it's good.

3 cans plop-fill, drained	various flavor gels, your choice

1. Form ploppers by hand. Each plopper should be about the shape of a human kneecap to make the proper *plop* sound when plopped into liquid.

2. Using your flavor EpiPen (epinephrine auto injector), stab flavor directly into middle of plopper. It needs to be the exact middle. Missing it by just a centimeter will destroy the plopper. You should be sweaty, shaking, and yelling at people to "Quiet down!" when trying to do this.

3. Pile ploppers on top of each other, separating each plopper with a single sheet of loose-leaf notebook paper. Place huge pile in

the bottom of your largest bulk freezer for 22 minutes, or until the loose-leaf paper feels cold to the finger touch.

4. Pile stack into tall oven and heat at 600 degrees until the skin of the ploppers is bubbling up with blisters. Remove ploppers and spread over serving dish in the pattern of a yin-yang, which is a Chinese symbol that describes nature's contrasting forces.

BONDI TITO!!

"PLEASE PASS THE MASHED POTATOES, AND DO SO WITH EQUANIMITY."

—*Gandhi,* ACTIVIST

Six
Hot Dog
Wieners

When we are struck with major bouts of depression, we often find that our refrigerator is left with nothing more than an already-opened package of hot dog wieners. But we've learned to never let this prevent us from cooking a meal and even having a little fun. Six hot dog wieners can not only feed you, but they can provide you with that slight boost of fun that will eventually elevate you from the immense depths of your inner tumult.

6 hot dog wieners

1. Remove hot dog wieners from packaging.
2. Hold a wiener between thumb and blaming finger and let dangle. With other hand, flick bottom of wiener so it swings back and forth a bit.
3. Grab wiener firmly in hand. Squeeze.
4. Roll wiener with hand back and forth over countertop.

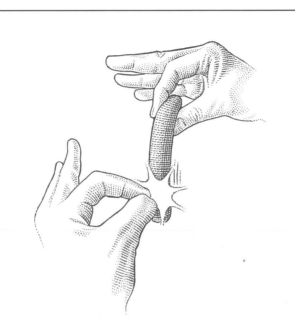

5. Use wiener to pretend to smoke a cigar. Do Groucho Marx impression for nobody.

6. Tuck wiener under curled-up upper lip. Wiener mustache.

7. Take two wieners at once and drum on table. Try drumming Ringo's solo from the last track on *Abbey Road*.

8. Lick wiener as though you just finished rolling a fat blunt. Then remember that this blunt one is kind of similar to the cigar one. Feel unoriginal. Let feeling pass.

9. Eat hot dog wieners.

BONDI TITO!!

DID YOU KNOW: **The initial construction of New York's Chrysler Building included a giant forty-foot mustard stain because its architect was eating a hot dog and accidentally dropped some mustard on the blueprints.**

Degrounded Puregrass

DRICKLED WITH
MORTON'S POOLSIDE SALTS

*During the summer, many people choose to do their cooking out-
side. It's a good way to connect with nature and cook outside.*

1 lawn (100 percent Merion Bluegrass) **1 fist-size rock Morton's Poolside Salt**	**1 baby's hat rosekarn**

1. Kneeling on lawn, use a trowel to churn grass and soil. This should loosen the grass blades and ruin the earth underneath.

2. Collect grass in a wheelbarrow.

3. Dump grass in a pool. The pool filter will catch all the good grass. Collect the wet mushy grass from the filter. That's the stuff you want to eat. The rest is nasty. You can eat it, but it's nasty.

4. Shave off some salt slivers and drickle onto degrounded puregrass.

5. Drickle a little rosekarn on top for stench.

6. Walk away.

BONDI TITO!!

Devil's
Meatcup

Everyone deserves the chance to indulge once in a while! And this dish definitely delivers in the indulgence department. It is one of our richest and tastiest morsels we've ever created. But all good things come at a price. We won't deny the presence of the actual devil in the making of this dish. When you decide to make this recipe, Satan himself will emerge from hell to help you make it. Indulge in the devilishly delicious Devil's Meatcup!

2 cups naked polenta	2 big wads ground round beef from cursed cow
15 big spoons sweet, soft, innocent, little butter	1 thong shredded whore's Parmesan
½ of 2 onions, pricked until chopped	4 tight chicken thighs
a bunch of other vegetables (it doesn't matter)	8 ramekins

1. Drown polenta in water in large pot and heat with increasing levels of hatred until polenta is cold and lifeless. Set aside.

CONTINUED

2. Melt butter in an antique skillet that once belonged to a disgraced priest.

3. When butter has melted down, throw in onions and whatever stupid vegetables you picked. We don't care about your vegetable garden so stop bringing it up.

4. When onions have started to look like they are crossing over to the dark side, add beef. Beef will start to roar and whisper. You will not have to do anything else to the beef in the pan at this point, as the devil will have taken over.

5. When roaring dies down to a whimper, remove from heat. Fill each ramekin halfway with the meat mixture and top with dead polenta and whored Parmesan.

6. Bake in the oven. Roaring will begin again. When windows begin opening and closing uncontrollably and your home is filled with the frigid winds of the underworld, meatcups are ready.

NOTE: Serving with grayed chicken spikes will deliver them from evil.

---

7. For chicken spikes, bake tight, sexy thighs until dry and spiky.

8. Shred into spikier pieces and leave out until gray. This could take several weeks, and by that time you may have forgotten why you left the chicken thighs out in the first place. Try not to forget, or you shall heed the devil's wrath.

BONDI TITO!!

DID YOU KNOW: Satan hates deviled eggs.

"UH-HUH."

—*Elvis Presley,* ON BEING ASKED IF HE WANTED
SECONDS ON POLENTA

HOW TO GET SOMEONE TO SHUT UP ABOUT THEIR VEGETABLE GARDEN

THESE TIPS ALSO WORK GREAT FOR getting people to shut up about other things.

1.

Stomp on the person's foot.

2.

Run away from the person.

3.

Pull a small frog out of your pocket to change the subject.

4.

Scream in the person's ear until they either run away or your voice goes hoarse.

5.

Using a common sewing kit, quickly thread a needle and sew the lips of the person talking about their vegetable garden shut.

Floury Crisper Crumbs

1 cup buttermilk
1⅓ cups nonfat milk
¼ cup hot sauce
2 cups all-purpose flour
1 cup cornmeal
1 cup water
¾ stick butter (6 tablespoons), cut into small chunks, then melted
1 tablespoon sugar
½ cup quick-cooking oats
⅛ teaspoon salt
⅛ teaspoon pepper
1 cup eggs (about 4 large eggs and 2 whites)
½ cinnamon stick
¼ teaspoon ground nutmeg
1½-inch piece fresh ginger, peeled and thinly sliced into matchstick pieces (about ¼ cup)
2 tablespoons pure maple syrup
1 tablespoon rice wine vinegar

¼ teaspoon red pepper flakes
2½ teaspoons paprika
1 tablespoon dried oregano
2 cloves garlic, thinly sliced
1 small red onion, halved and sliced root to stem
1½ cups white sugar
2 teaspoons baking powder
½ teaspoon baking soda
¼ teaspoon almond extract
½ teaspoon vanilla extract
1 tablespoon grated orange zest
¼ cup flax-seed meal
⅓ cup canola oil
powdered sugar, for topping
½ cup chopped walnuts (optional)
3 large Jonagold or Gala apples, peeled, cored and cut into ½-inch-thick slices (optional)

1. Mix ingredients.
2. Cook ingredients.

FOOD
GREATS

FOOD GREATS PRAYER

*Food Greats, great food, we think of you now as we prepare
to devour you. May you fill our stomachs and not give our
scarred and shredded bodies diarrhea this time.* **AMEN.**

Dead Dog

CO-PLATED WITH YAM CLIPPINGS AND
A LEAFY SAGE DUMPING

This is one of our favorite recipes to make. It's one of our least favorite dishes to eat, though. Weird.

～ SERVES: 1 ～

1 dog (dead)	**1** black trash bag
19 peppy grunds	water (to fill bag)
construction salt (to taste)	**1** bad thought
2 heroin spoons pigeon oil	**1** competent garbageman
1 bag Russet potatoes	**1** package glitter
1 small can red paint	**1** package stickers
3 pounds sage leaves	

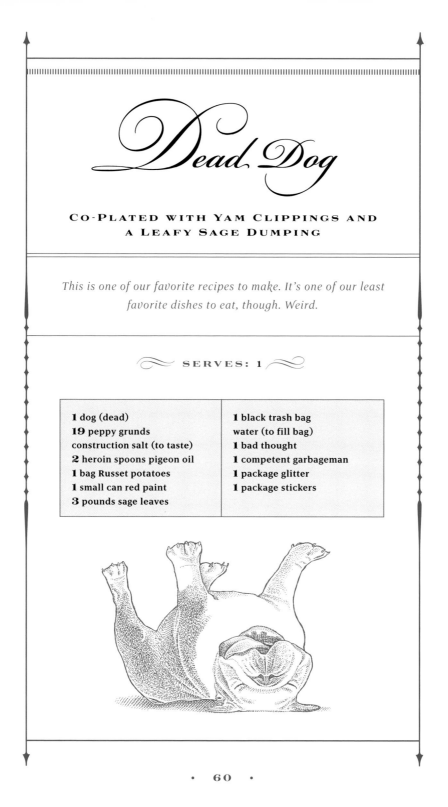

1. To prepare dead dog, purchase a dead dog and remove it from its bag.

2. Rub down with peppy grunds and construction salt.

3. Pan-sizzle with pigeon oil until it starts to smell bad.

4. Yams can be very expensive, so paint Russet potatoes red to trick people.

5. Clip up potatoes with garden shears. If you don't have garden shears, you can steal them from a neighbor who never uses them anyway.

6. For leafy sage dumping, become upset by thinking of something that angers you. (We always use the way Japanese-Americans were treated during World War II. Use whatever makes *you* angry, like the fact that you just can't seem to lose any weight no matter how many times you try adjusting your eating habits.)

7. When fully irate, hand-rip sage leaves into black trash bag and fill with water. Tie up bag and let sit overnight outdoors.

8. To serve, slam dead dog onto plate. Pin corsage of yam clippings onto dog's lapel.

9. Invite competent garbageman into your home and make him dump the whole load of leafy sage on and around the plate.

10. Decorate the dog's cute tail with glitter and stickers.

BUMPI TINTO!!

DID YOU KNOW: Sage was invented in 1968, three years after Simon and Garfunkel used the nonsense word *sage* in their song "Scarborough Fair." Everyone thought that it should be a spice, so they made it into one.

HOW TO FIND
A COMPETENT GARBAGEMAN

1.

Set up an audition. Visit your local casting website and check off the box that says "Garbagemen."

2.

Set up a time for the garbagemen to arrive at your house. Three o'clock P.M. always works great for us!

3.

During each audition, have garbagemen improvise different funny trash situations. Whoever makes you laugh the most is the funniest garbageman.

4.

Do not pick the funniest garbageman.

5.

Pick the most competent garbageman.

Clumps of Turkey

IN A BED OF HEAVY TOMATO SCUM
WITH SOFTENED RICE POLES

As small children, we were dropped off at an Indian reservation in a remote location and left there for twelve days. We were never given an explanation for why we were dropped off there, but we were luckily taken in by an old woman whose children were grown up. She fed us and let us stay in her children's old beds. We even wore their old clothing. We thought she was nice but we were really relieved to leave the reservation when our parents came back.

1 pound ground turkey	1 block cream cheese
1 glop pigeon oil	2 children's handfuls gray and black rocks
4 sets of identical-twin tomatoes	2 snack bags hard rice poles
1 floor	

1. Rip-n-smush up turkey into big clumps. Place clumps evenly on wax paper. Take a picture for your lame food blog.

CONTINUED

2. Squirt a glop of pigeon oil onto a big, hot, flat surface. We recommend something like a pan that you could buy at a store.

3. Cook clumps on pan for just long enough so they don't burn, occasionally flipping them so you have something to do.

4. Meanwhile, drop tomatoes onto floor. Remove big chunks of tomato from floor and throw them into the trash. (For more on throwing things into the trash, read a book about it.)

5. Leave the squished little red bitches there for several days so they get real scummy. Eventually scrape up scum and put it on a plate.

6. Shit cream cheese from package. Add rocks for heaviness.

7. For softened rice poles, just make like you normally would.

8. The recipe is done. You don't have to read or do any more.

9. Move on to the next thing in your life.

BUNZI TIFTO!!

"I'M TOTALLY A CEREAL-FOR-DINNER WOMAN."

—*Albert Einstein*, PHYSICIST

Prussian-Style Beach Oats

SAT ON BY SOUR JUICE, BIPPIES, AND HAYSTACK SEEDS (OPTIONAL)

Some recipes are meant to be open to the reader's interpretation. A dish as simple as Prussian-style beach oats should be made the way you would enjoy them . . . or not! Have fun, relax, and just go for it (optional)!

2 cups water (optional)	**1** package multiflavored extra big bippies (optional)
1 pinch salt (optional)	**1** pile haystack seeds (optional)
1 sack Prussian-style beach oats (optional)	**1** teaspoon honey
1 tablespoon sour juice (optional)	

1. Bring lightly salted water to a boil (optional).

2. Mix in beach oats (completely optional). (If you don't want to eat oats right now, that's up to you. Or if you want them but don't feel like making them, have someone else do it or just make them another time.)

3. Cook for 5 minutes. (Again, this is totally optional. Maybe you like burnt oats. We don't know you, so cook it as long as you want, or

CONTINUED

don't cook it at all. No need to feel pressure to make this recipe if you're not feelin' it or whatever.)

4. Remember to stir while cooking. (Or not. NO BIG DEAL! Stirring is optional. If you like clumps or just don't feel like stirring, don't bother, man. We cool? Cool.)

5. (Letting the oats sit to cool would normally be listed here as step number 5, but we don't want to force that on you. We're not like that. In fact, let's say don't worry about this step at all and just go do something else entirely. *Law & Order: SVU* is probably on, so you could watch that. Unless you don't want to [optional]).

6. Looking at step number 6 is 100 percent optional. Close your eyes or look somewhere else, if that's what you'd prefer. Looking out the window is cool, and you can always look at a wall, but that feels like too much pressure. Listen, if you're still making the oats—which, again, is totally your call—then top it off with some sour juice, or bippies, or haystack seeds, or anything you want, really. Hell, you could top it with hot sauce or something crazy like that, but that's just us spitballing. This is about you. Just, like, do it your way, ya know?

7. Add a touch of honey. This step you have to do. Or we're calling the police.

BINI MINI!!

"E.T. EAT PIZZA."

—*E.T.*, ALIEN

Round-Eye Flank Stringers

WITH YANKEE-POISONED MARINARA AND FUZZY RICE CURDS

By now, you've learned that some recipes are easy to make. You can just dump a bunch of food together, mix it around, and voilà! You've made something that, technically, you can eat. Other recipes, however, require extreme commitment, focus, courage, precision, equanimity, resilience, and strength of character. Like this one.

SERVES: 3X *if* X = 19θ

π tablespoons red wine vinegar	32 oz. flank steak
$2/17$ cup marinara sauce	.23582 cups basmati rice
-2.5 mg sea salt	2.45 cloves garlic
.0451 mg peppy grunds	40 decimeters² Yankee Poison
$3/7$ cup olive oil	

CONTINUED

1. ∞ f(red wine vinegar)9(marinara sauce)

2. Σ = _____ (2ø˚peppy grunds - olive oil)n!

3. (Flank Steak = 0) (basmati rice) X n

4. n! = marinara sauce X Vinegar^3/Water = Garlic^3/Θ cups = Yankee Poison

5. ΣRice$_m$2/(-27 rice curds)$^\Theta$(6 cups x marinara)^2

6. Σ x m = 1 serving

BUNNA MICHO!!

"IF ALL THE HUNGRY PEOPLE WERE GIVEN MEALS, THEY WOULD NO LONGER BE HUNGRY."

—Mark Twain, AUTHOR

Cheese-Meat Lazanni for Twelve

Cooking for a big group of people can be stressful, but fear not. It's basically the same as cooking for yourself, except there's a lot more stuff involved and it's much more difficult. But soldiering through adversity will make you better. Have you ever met an adult who was bullied as a child? They are much cooler people now. Or sometimes they are much worse people specifically because of all the bullying. Bad example.

1 pound lazanni noodles	**2 cloves garlic**
1 pound spicy Italian sausage	**4 onions**
¾ pound ground beef	**4 cans crushed tomatoes**

1. Bring a pot of salted water to boil.

2. Add lazanni noodles to boiling water. Realize midway that they don't fit because you never picked up the large pot from your ex's apartment and this one isn't big enough.

CONTINUED

3. Rummage through pots. Find one that's almost big enough, and then pour some of the boiling water into it and also drop in excess noodles, causing water to spill all over stovetop.

4. With a hand towel, wipe spilled water off stovetop. Quickly throw hand towel into the sink as soon as it catches fire.

5. As fire alarm goes off, open windows, turn on fans, and repeatedly open and close front door.

6. Remember that you should've cooked the meat first.

7. Yell, "Goddammit!"

8. Throw some oil into a pan. Any pan. It doesn't matter at this point. Just get something hot.

9. While shaking with anxiety, rip meat from packaging, causing several sausages to drop onto your dirty kitchen floor.

10. Blow off hair and dust. Run sausages under faucet.

11. Since you forgot to set a timer, now seems as good a time as any to strain the noodles.

12. Scream as the steam from the water scalds your face.

13. Toss meat, garlic, and onions into oiled pan. There's definitely not enough time to chop up the onions but ripping them up a little will be fine. No one's gonna say anything. They better not.

14. Scream again as the piping-hot oil blisters your skin.

15. Lay stuck-together noodles in the baking pan. It won't look good, but it's just food, right? It's all gonna look the same on the way out.

16. Remember that you completely forgot to buy cheese. Slap forehead.

17. Head out to the corner store. All they have is sliced low-fat Swiss, but at this point, that's good enough. It's white, it's cheese, it's fine. Buy two packages and a bottle of Diet Coke because there is a ten-dollar credit-card minimum. Start arguing with cashier about the minimum. Tell him you don't have time for this, but really you're just upset because he's winning the argument.

18. Dump cans of crushed tomatoes, cheese slices, and burnt meat (you burned the meat) onto noodles. Repeat making layers until you run out of cheese slices.

19. Bake for like 2 hours since you didn't preheat the oven. Idiot.

20. Get angry that none of your friends ever cook for you.

21. Remove baking dish from oven. Scream as pan burns your hand.

22. Remember that the dinner is actually scheduled for tomorrow.

BOMO MIPPO!!

"I WILL NOT TRY GOAT CHEESE. I HAVE NO INTEREST."

—*Susan B. Anthony,*
WOMEN'S RIGHTS ACTIVIST

Chef's Nook

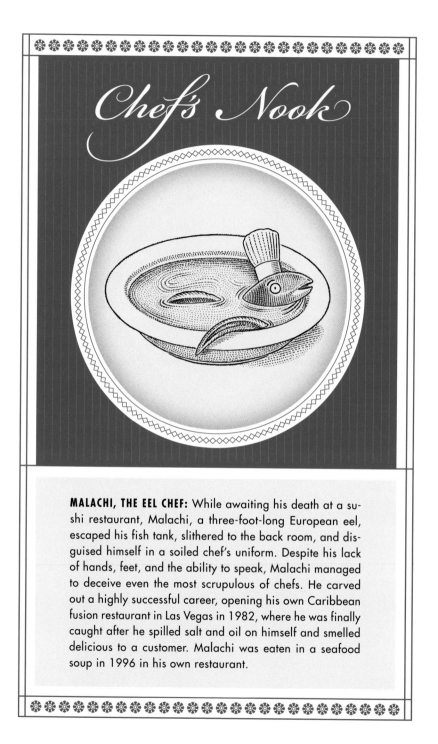

MALACHI, THE EEL CHEF: While awaiting his death at a sushi restaurant, Malachi, a three-foot-long European eel, escaped his fish tank, slithered to the back room, and disguised himself in a soiled chef's uniform. Despite his lack of hands, feet, and the ability to speak, Malachi managed to deceive even the most scrupulous of chefs. He carved out a highly successful career, opening his own Caribbean fusion restaurant in Las Vegas in 1982, where he was finally caught after he spilled salt and oil on himself and smelled delicious to a customer. Malachi was eaten in a seafood soup in 1996 in his own restaurant.

Chicken Francese

THAT'S ACTUALLY JUST RICE

Saving money is very important, especially when you're four months behind in rent like we are. So sometimes to save money on the meals we're making for dinner parties, we like to trick people into thinking we are making a complicated dish, when in fact we are just using rice for everything.

1 30-pound bag of rice some water stray pigeon feathers	small cardboard boxes (stolen)

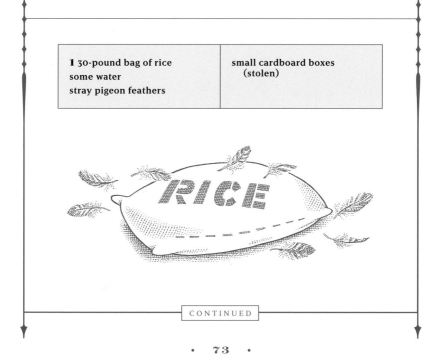

CONTINUED

1. Make sure you're alone and no one will be coming home for like an hour.

2. Overcook rice and form into the shape of chicken breasts. Rice is cheaper than chicken.

3. Instead of flour, put some rice in a bowl and instead of salt and pepper, mix it with rice and more rice. Rice is actually cheaper than flour, salt, and pepper.

4. Instead of beating the eggs, beat the rice (which is cheaper than eggs) with 3 tablespoons of water (which is free). Heat over a medium-high rice flame (to avoid paying a higher gas bill).

5. Dip both sides of the rice cutlets in the rice-rice-rice mix, along with the rice and water. Steam for 2 minutes and hope that it starts looking more like chicken somehow.

6. Stick some stray pigeon feathers from down the block into the rice. People will think it's chicken because chickens have feathers.

7. Serve meal inside small boxes, each labeled CHICKEN FRANCESE: MADE WITH REAL CHICKEN, so people have to see that before eating it.

8. Remove rice concoction from boxes, look at everyone, and say, "Bock bock bock! Right, guys?"

9. Turn on the stereo and have it cued up to "The Chicken Dance." Say out loud, "Whoa, that's so weird! Cuz we're eating chicken!" Make everyone do the chicken dance.

BONGO CORTO!!

"MAN, I'M STUFFED."

—Jimi Hendrix, ROCK MUSICIAN

Shitty Chicken

SPANKED WITH CINNAMON-GARLIC DIRT AND DIMPLED WITH A FRESHWATER WHALE-TIT SAUCE

We remember being kids, and our mom would cook for us all the time. She never made this recipe.

～ SERVES: 2 ～

PREPARATION TIME: 9½ YEARS

2 old, shitty chicken breasts	1 chunky cup garlic powder
1 bad attitude	1 spit natural cellar dirt powder
1 thing of receipt paper	
2 cups Original Flavor™ water	1 squirt of whale tit
1 pantload cinnamon powder	1 old, shitty chicken head

1. To shitify chicken, do not feed it properly. Ignore it as much as possible, and make fun of it behind its back. (A good mean thing to do to a chicken is to push it down for no reason.*)

2. Use your bad attitude to lie to the chicken at any opportunity (e.g., tell the chicken it's a Friday when really it's Monday).

* For other ideas of mean things to do to a chicken, please read Dumping Gatorade on a Chicken and 1,001 Other Mean Things to Do to a Chicken *by John Grisham.*

CONTINUED

3. Following the slaughter, wrap the chicken meat in receipt paper and throw it into the refrigerator using a sharp, overhand baseball throw.

4. To cook, put Original Flavor™ water over high heat to boil and granny-toss the chicken in for as long as it takes to cook.

5. For cinnamon-garlic dirt, mix three powders in huge wooden bowl.

NOTE: We like to pronounce the word *huge* with a silent letter *H* so it sounds more like *yuge*.

---

6. Spank dirt onto the shitty chicken with two solid dump-thrusts.

7. Take whale tit firmly in your fists and squirt directly from tit to plate, otherwise it doesn't count.

8. Using your mid-knuckle, dimple sauce into chicken.

9. Garnish with old chicken head (so people know what animal they're eating).

BUNCHO PEEPO!!

"I'M A SIMPLE MAN, I LIKE SIMPLE THINGS. I LIKE FRENCH FRIES MORE THAN ONION RINGS."

—Dwight D. Eisenhower,
U.S. PRESIDENT

HOW TO
OBTAIN A WHALE TIT

1.

Purchase a modest whaling vessel.

2.

Hire crew of wandering sailors.

3.

Train sailors for the whaling voyage. They're all a little rusty.

4.

Hunt and kill whale.

5.

With the help of the sailors and a friend's Dodge Ram, drag dead whale to fresh body of water and let sit for 7 days (this is how long it takes for a saltwater animal to become a freshwater animal).

6.

Now that your crew of sailors is no longer employed, find families in your neighborhood that they can stay with. They helped you; it is only fair that you help them.

7.

The whale's tit is located where tits usually are. It is now ready for use.

"LEAVES OF GRASS. SCOOPS OF ICE CREAM."

—*Walt Whitman*, POET

Chicken Ethylene Oxide

To most people, food appears to be just solids and liquids. To the Mizretti Brothers (us), food can also be gaseous, invisible, or what we call "antifood," which is, simply put, the opposite of food. Here is a recipe for a delicious gaseous meal, which does require some tremendous personal risk. Make this recipe . . . ¡if you got the balls for it, hombre!

1 pound's worth fresh-hacked chicken	**1 50-pound tank ethylene oxide gas**

1. In stepdad's garage, tear up chicken and stuff bits into 8-inch stainless-steel pipe.
2. Install a valve and a gas regulator leading from gas tank to pipe.
3. Place a valve on the pipe going to the main reactor.
4. Load pipe with ethylene oxide gas and set aflame.
5. A colorless, flammable gas with a faintly sweet odor will emerge. Use an empty 2-liter soda bottle to collect the gas.
6. Hold thumb over top of soda bottle to keep gas inside.

CONTINUED

7. As soon as you are ready for this, place mouth over soda bottle and inhale chicken gas.

8. Keep going, dude.

9. You're almost there. Finish it off, bro, finish it off.

10. You fuckin' DID IT! You fuckin' just inhaled chicken gas!

11. Tell your friends.

BEEPI JEEPO!!

DID YOU KNOW: **If you rearrange the letters in "kcienhc," it spells "chicken."**

"HELLO? YES, I'D LIKE TO ORDER SOME CHINESE FOOD."

—*Alexander Graham Bell,* INVENTOR

Secret Item

WITH SURPRISE BAG

4 ??????	????????
???????	**2** ???
???	?
2 t ??????	**1** burlap bag with 2 big
?????	question marks on the
	sides of the bag

1. Take the ???? and ?????? for 15 ???.

2. Let the ?????? ????? for ??? hours.

3. Preheat oven to 350 ??????.

4. Twist and squeeze ????? forcefully into ????????.

5. ???????????????????

6. ???

7. ????? ????????? ?? ???????????? 30 ????.

8. ??? ??? ?? ??? ??? ?? ??? ??? ??.

9. ?? ?? ?? ?? ?? ?? ?? ?? ??

10. Place in bag. Serve.

POOFI SCORCHO!!

St. Louis–Style Barbeque Ribs

WITH LOW-FAT GARLIC-DILL MASHED POTATOES AND FRESH VEGETABLE STUFFING

About fifteen years ago, we were driving from Orlando, Florida, to Carson City, Nevada, when we became hungry along the way. We stopped at a Boston Market just off I-40. The meal was incredible. And that's when we came to a stunning realization: Anything can be a recipe as long as you list a few ingredients and some steps for how to make it. And this was a meal that we loved so very much that we decided to call it our own recipe.

1 car	13 American dollars

1. Drive to Boston Market. Check bostonmarket.com for the nearest location.

2. Get in line. Make sure to assert your position. Don't just stand in the middle of two lines and confuse everyone.

3. While waiting, look at the menu and decide what to get. Base this decision on foods that you have liked in the past.

4. When it's your turn to order, say, "Um, hi, yeah, can I get the

St. Louis–style BBQ ribs? And for my sides, let's see . . . I'll have the mashed potatoes, and, I guess the, um . . . the vegetable stuffing?"

5. Smile a little. Be confident in your order.

6. Hand cashier American dollars.

7. Take receipt and say "Thank you."

8. Get food and walk it to your car.

9. On the way to the car, throw the receipt in the trash.

10. Drive home fast, making sure to open the box and eat some of the food on your way home.

KIPSI MITO!!

DID YOU KNOW: The longest a pizza delivery ever took was four weeks. Three people died.

Crab Dorks

WITH SOMETHING ELSE ON IT

We remember being kids.

900 dead crabs	**1** cup karnmeal
2 eggs	**1** fat man's thumb's worth of oil
½ cup White Power sugar	**1** something else
1 cup flaür	

1. In huge, heavy pot, steam all 900 dead crabs for 5 minutes.

2. Once cooked, plunge out crabmeat with crab plunger.

3. Pile crabmeat on plate. Look at it. Smile.

4. From 20 feet away, basketball-shoot eggs, sugar, flaür, and karnmeal into a mixing bowl. Make appropriate crowd-cheering sounds with mouth.

5. Mix dem 'gredients.

6. Dorkle crab meat into 20 separate dorks. Dork-dip them into batter.

7. Heat a fat man's thumb's worth of oil to 385 degrees. Dunk dorks in. Crowd goes wild.

8. Cook in big batches to just get it over with. Cooking is annoying when it goes slowly. Serve hot as hell.

9. For "something else," place something else on the plate, like a big leaf or a piece of copper wire. Don't feel the need to be too creative, as no one gives a shit about this part of the meal since they're not gonna eat it.

ZINO PAPO!!

"MAN, WHAT A GREAT DINNER."

—*Bruce Springsteen,* ROCK MUSICIAN

Triton-Based Turms

WITH GRISTLE SPRAY AND A PEACH DORD

We still remember being kids.

SERVES: 2 TO 3

PREPARATION TIME: 7 YEARS, 10 HOURS

1 seal's tummy triton sludge	**6** large blue-whale tailbones
8 small turms	**1** live elephant's spinal fluid
2 scrimps mercury oil	**2** peaches

1. Reduce triton sludge over low heat in wok for 6 to 8 hours. Slam-dunk turms into sludge, add mercury oil, and allow to slip-slide until fully covered and glazed. The smell in the kitchen should be horrible.

2. Travel to India and befriend an elephant. Take years to slowly earn his trust.

3. In seventh year of elephant friendship, tell elephant to look behind him. When elephant has his back turned, coldheartedly stab elephant with syringe and extract spinal fluid.

4. Run back home.

5. For gristle spray, pull out gristle from tailbones and blend until smooth. Pour into spray can and spray away! Don't even worry about spraying the food; this part's about having fun.

6. For peach dord, refuse to clip your fingernails for 3 weeks.

7. Shred 2 big, soft peaches with unclipped fingernails and form one large dord. Can be heated, eaten cold, or looked at from across the room.

SKIVI STITO!!

"MY BIGGEST
WEAKNESS IN LIFE HAS
ALWAYS BEEN GROCERY-STORE
BIRTHDAY CAKES."

—*John Lennon*, MUSICIAN

HOW TO
GAIN AN ELEPHANT'S TRUST

1.

Do things to make the elephant like you, such as giving him big leaves to eat or washing his ass.

2.

Tell the elephant funny, elephant-related jokes. (Sample joke: Q: What time is it when an elephant sleeps in your bed? A: Time to buy a new bed!)

3.

Make fun of the other animals in the savannah.

4.

Share a very personal secret with the elephant that no one else knows. (Sample secret: One time, I told my friend that my dad invented sloppy joes.)

5.

Show the elephant an embarrassing part of your body that no one else knows about. (Sample body part: that embarrassing tree growing out of your inner thigh.)

6.

Ask the elephant to trust you.

Bill Clinton Sandwich

Self-explanatory.

Pocoloquitos-Style Meat Saucers

FORCED INTO A CHEDDAR COFFIN
SERVED OVER A PILE OF BONES
(NOT GOOD)

Throw on a pair of baggy jeans, an XXL baseball jersey, and an upside-down visor. Drive your car around real fast, drink a large cup of soda, litter, and generally disregard basic laws. You are now living Pocoloquitos style and are ready to cook this meat.

PREPARATION TIME: 16 HOURS

SERVES: 0
(NO ONE SHOULD EAT THIS.
IT'S TERRIBLE.)

2 meat	**55** blocks of cheddar
1 regulation-size ultimate Frisbee	**1** rodent-size pet casket
2 spice clouds	**1** pet owl (optional)

1. Squish meat (2) into bottom of Frisbee.

2. Sprinkle salt, pepper, garlic, and whatever other spices you have

lying around into your mouth. Swish them around a bit and cough the spice cloud onto the meat. Remove meat from Frisbee. Flip over. Repeat.

DON'T FORGET: Get someone else to clean up whatever spices went all over the place!

---

3. Place Frisbee into preheated oven. Meat is done baking when house stinks like burnt Frisbee.

4. For cheddar coffin, get blocks of cheddar hot (with fire?). Drop coffin into cheese and then quickly scare the cheese so that it freezes in shock and retains its shape.

5. Chisel tiny cross onto the top layer of the coffin so you know you're eating the right religion.

6. Close your eyes and cram meat into the coffin. If the meat is sticking out in weird places and parts of the coffin are broken, then you've done it right.

7. Bones are easy to find if you don't take care of your home and mice die in there. Or simply ask your pet owl to give you the bones of the mice he's recently murdered. Most pet owls will do this no problem. (As a third option, you may steal the bones off a fat man's plate at a local tavern.)

8. Scatter collected bones on dirty plate. Place meat-stuffed coffin on top. Now it's ready to serve!

HOMMO BEEFO!!

WHERE TO
GET BONES

1.

Buried in a giant pyramid

2.

Bone store

3.

Ask your friend Ryan if he has any lying around

4.

Dog's mouth

5.

Museum (kill an animal there and take its bones)

"WE JUST TOOK
OUR FIRST AIRPLANE RIDE.
THE FOOD WAS OKAY."

—*The Wright brothers,* INVENTORS

Cheese and Fish

a bunch of cheese	a bunch of fish

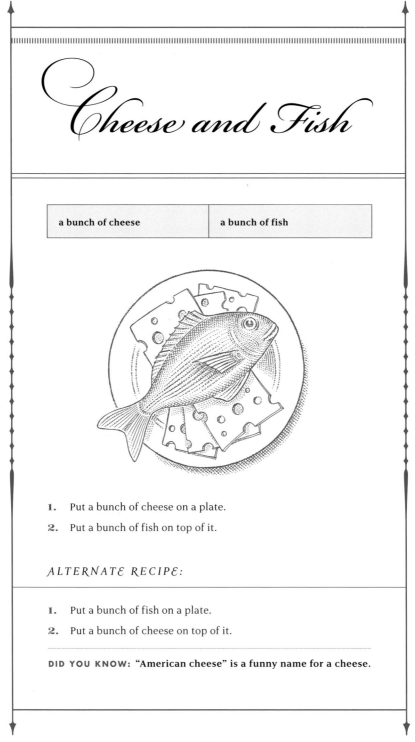

1. Put a bunch of cheese on a plate.
2. Put a bunch of fish on top of it.

ALTERNATE RECIPE:

1. Put a bunch of fish on a plate.
2. Put a bunch of cheese on top of it.

DID YOU KNOW: "American cheese" is a funny name for a cheese.

Chef's Nook

THE CHEF WHO BROKE THE COLOR BARRIER: In 1941, Jackson Roberts became the first African-American chef in the United States. He was hired by the owner of Rick's Steakhouse, Rick Doldgrin, who really wanted to hire a black chef so he would be written about in books like this one. According to sources, Roberts was forced to deal with an abundance of hostility and pressure. Surprisingly, none of it was race-related—it was just a very busy restaurant.

HRAK

HRAK PRAYER

Hrak, O Hrak. Thou sustaineth me. Thou keepeth my belly full. Thou haveth protein. Thou maketh a good leftover. Thou art thou. Thou art Hrak. Hrak art thou. **AMEN.**

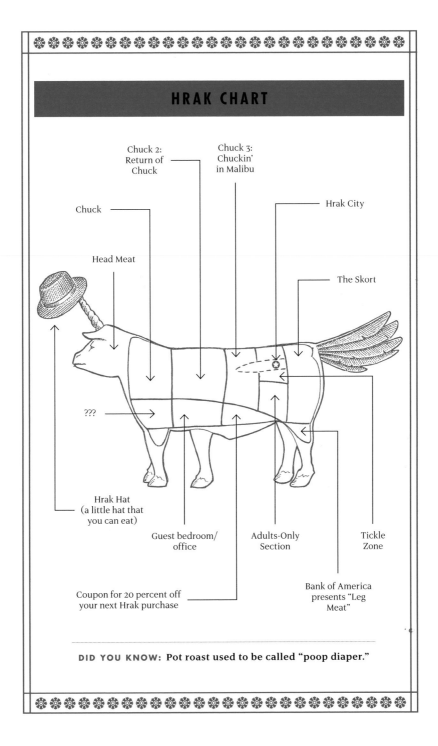

HRAK CHART

Chuck 2:
Return of
Chuck

Chuck 3:
Chuckin'
in Malibu

Chuck

Hrak City

Head Meat

The Skort

???

Hrak Hat
(a little hat that
you can eat)

Guest bedroom/
office

Adults-Only
Section

Tickle
Zone

Coupon for 20 percent off
your next Hrak purchase

Bank of America
presents "Leg
Meat"

- -

DID YOU KNOW: Pot roast used to be called **"poop diaper."**

Polished Windhog

TICKLED WITH A STEAMED BUTTER-SPANIEL SAUCE

It's important to put love into all your dishes, because if you don't love your food, people will notice and then they'll yell at you. So always make sure to care for your food, hold it, kiss it, argue with it, cry with it, kick it out of your house, let it back in, and share an even deeper connection with it afterward. And yes, putting love into your food technically violates several health codes.

3 medium-size butter sculptures of cocker spaniels **⅓** pound windhog, drained of blood	**1** fingering of medium-brown boot cream **1** handful of greenies **½** clop water

1. Take days to painstakingly mold butter into three lifelike sculptures of lovable cocker spaniels. Really fall in love with them as though they're real and not butter.

2. Place butter sculptures in a large pot along with water clop like

you're going to give your babies a bath. Place over low heat and cover with translucent lid.

3. Watch through the lid as your sweet spaniels melt into nothing. The sauce will be ready, and you will be stronger for this.

4. Rub down white, lifeless windhog with boot cream until fully coated and glistening like a new boot. Let boot cream polish sit for 3 hours.

5. Broil for 10 minutes until windhog is a little bit hot. Meanwhile, finely chop greenies and dip their tips into the butter-spaniel sauce.

6. Remove windhog and then, with light, dainty motions, flicker the sauce onto the windhog until it's been fully tickled. Repeat until it looks like the windhog is smiling. Then serve.

MISO BINACA!!

"TO REALLY KNOW SOMEONE, YOU SHOULD GO INTO HIS HOUSE AND EAT WITH HIM. YOU'LL FIND OUT WHAT THAT PERSON'S HOUSE LOOKS LIKE AND WHAT THEY LIKE TO EAT."

—*Carl Jung,* PSYCHOLOGIST

Frautéed Bull Joints

DUMPED IN A BUCKET'S WORTH OF
HUSH-PUPPY OIL PAINT. YOU ALSO GET
COINED CELERY AND RYAN'S RICE

We have not forgotten about being kids.

1 purebred rodeo bull	5 dimes (dirty or clean)
1 extra-large black garbage bag	20 stalks crunchy, good celery
1 extra-large Samsonite suitcase	2 Tupperware containers of Ryan's Rice
some pliers	1 Ryan
10 hush puppies	
1 gallon oil paint (Dark Khaki or Egyptian White)	

1. Catch a flight to San Antonio, Texas.

2. Book a two-night hotel stay.

3. Purchase one ticket to any San Antonio Stock Show and Rodeo Feb. 16–19 at AT&T Center San Antonio. After the show, stalk and kill the best bull.

4. Stealthily stuff bull into garbage bag. Stuff garbage bag into suitcase.

5. Catch a flight back home, being sure to check your suitcase. (After all, we don't want our slain bull to stink up the aircraft!)

6. Once at home and in your kitchen, remove the bull from the garbage bag. Using some pliers, remove bull's joints.

7. Using an Anderson mixer, mix together hush puppies and oil paint. Add in bull joints.

8. Frautée hush puppy–oil paint–bull joint mix for 20 minutes to 6 days.

9. Use dimes to coin the celery, being sure to clearly imprint Franklin Delano Roosevelt's image onto celery.

10. Call up Ryan. You know, Ryan. You guys have been friends since seventh grade. You used to play Super Bases Loaded on Super Nintendo. It's cool that you guys are still friends, even after that big fight you had junior year of college. Can you believe you guys fought like that? It was awful. One full hour of yelling that ended in tears. But it made you both better people, and it made your friendship stronger. Now you don't see each other as much anymore, but when you do, it's just like old times. You joke around, you connect . . . it's still real. And man, Ryan just makes the *best rice*. Tell him to grab his pickup truck and bring some of it over. You guys'll sit on the porch, knock a few down, and have a blast.

11. Tell Ryan to please leave.

CONO FUGAZI!!

DID YOU KNOW: We're having rice pilaf for dinner tonight.

"MAN, YOU GOTTA EAT FOOD."

—*Janis Joplin,* ROCK MUSICIAN

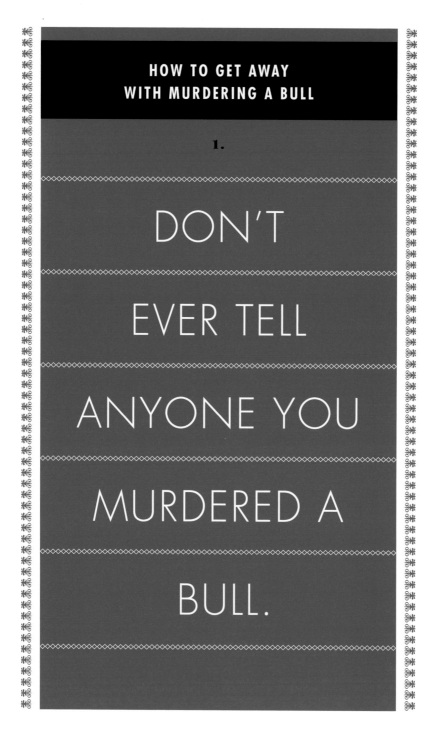

HOW TO GET AWAY WITH MURDERING A BULL

1.

DON'T EVER TELL ANYONE YOU MURDERED A BULL.

Braised Tenderhoof

WITH MINSTREL WINE DIPPING HERBS AND A CASHEW NECKLACE

Okay, so before we get to this recipe, can we just say something? We're sorry, but if you have a bicycle in the city—that's great, and, like, we get what you're doing, but you CANNOT take up a full lane of traffic. You have BIKE LANES! They are there for you to use. That having been said, here is our recipe for a delectable braised tenderhoof!

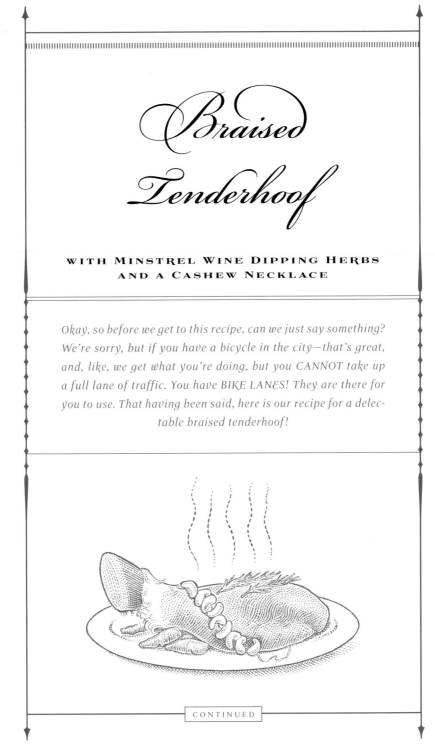

CONTINUED

1 tenderhoof **5** handfuls cashews **4** stalks predipped herbs **1** gold necklace	**2** breasts purple wine **1** mushed-up garlic pile **4** broken carrots

1. Let tenderhoof thaw for one hour.

2. All right, look. We can't drive our car in bike lanes without getting a ticket, which HAS happened, several times, when it wasn't even our fault! So you shouldn't be in our way when we have to be somewhere, okay?

3. Anyway. Braised tenderhoof. This is great for parties.

4. You know what? Sorry, one more thing about these skinny guys on bikes. They turn whenever they want! What rules are you following? You're making them up!

5. Place cashews into—listen, we are tolerant people. We like most people. We get along with like every kind of race and religion. But sometimes, these bikes, they're in the crosswalk. Sometimes they zip off the sidewalk and into oncoming traffic. That's ridiculous! You're the ones putting people in danger, and then you yell at us.

6. Oh my God. Anyway . . . tenderhoof . . .

7. Where are the cops on this bike thing? They do nothing but blame you when they didn't even see what happened!

8. Staying on this bike thing for a second, we remember this one time that we were stopped at a stoplight in the LEFT LANE. So the front door is slightly ajar, so we open it quickly so that we can close it. And as it's open, this skinny guy on a bike gets hit by the door. But we were in the LEFT LANE! So yes, our car door hit him, but WHY WAS HE NOT BIKING ON THE SIDE OF THE ROAD?!?! HE WAS IN THE MIDDLE OF THE STREET!!! And when the cops came, they blamed us!!! WHAT THE FUCK?!?

9. We're sorry, we don't feel like writing a recipe right now. Minstrel wine dipping herbs. A cashew necklace. You get it. It's not that hard. Why do you need a book for this? Just go do something else. Ugh.

"I DID NOT HAVE SEXUAL RELATIONS WITH [MONICA LEWINSKY]."

—*Bill Clinton*, U.S. PRESIDENT

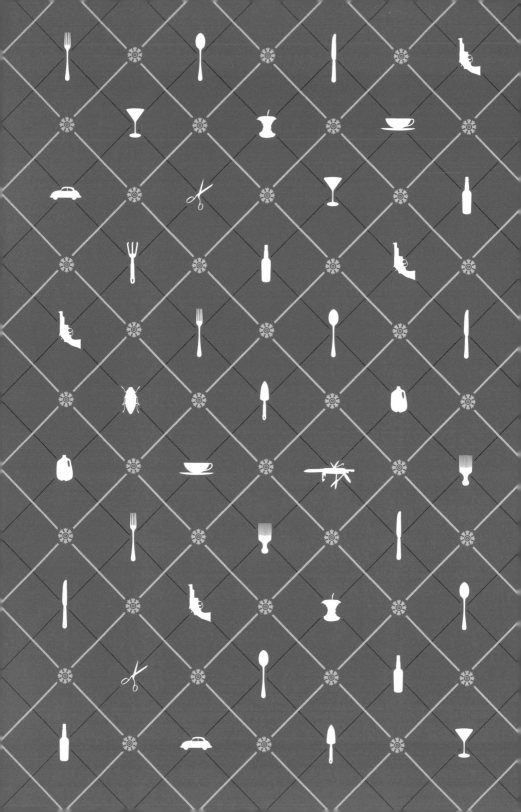

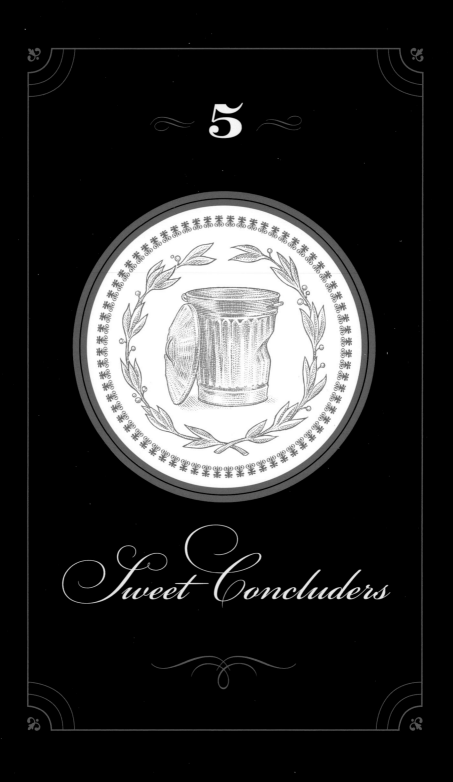

~ 5 ~

Sweet Concluders

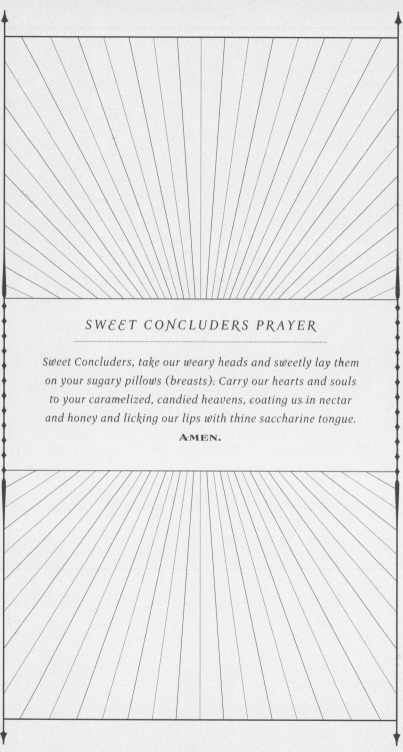

SWEET CONCLUDERS PRAYER

Sweet Concluders, take our weary heads and sweetly lay them on your sugary pillows (breasts). Carry our hearts and souls to your caramelized, candied heavens, coating us in nectar and honey and licking our lips with thine saccharine tongue.

AMEN.

Fat Cream Whores

KICKED OUT OF A BED OF PEAR OOZE

This one's so fucking good. Oh my God. So much sugar. So much butter and cream. It's incredible. Isn't it crazy how when you mix those things together it's like the most amazing thing ever? While eating this, you'll be tempted to ejaculate. Don't. You're supposed to ejaculate after a meal, not during. Sometimes you want the richest food available. Remember the triangle of rich dessert: cream, butter, and sugar.

10 whole, fat cream thighs	**2** soft green pears with black spots
6 little pats of well-mannered and courteous butter	so much sugar
3 two-yolk eggs with tiny blood spot in each	your own chapped, red fingers

1. Slice open thighs and empty cream into pan. Heat slowly until cream starts to thicken.

2. Melt little butter pats in the heated cream. This is the funnest part of the process because the butter is helpless and can't do anything about it. Stir as cream thickens further.

CONTINUED

3. In a bowl that is too small, mess up the eggs. Stop worrying about what spills out of the bowl. *Start letting go of worries like that more in your life and you'll be a happier person.* Pour the eggs into the thickening cream and continue stirring until fully incorporated.

4. In separate pan over low heat, scrape off pieces of pear with your fingers and add so much sugar (just don't stop).

5. Add more sugar.

6. Form cream mixture into whores about the size of a walnut. Use a dog's testicle as a reference for size.

7. Put a small plate on a larger plate, and spread ooze over the small plate to look like a shabby bed you'd make on the floor out of nasty blankets. Place 3 whores in bed and then shove them all out onto the larger plate. They will be lightly coated in ooze.

POGO STICKO!!

Raspberry Quintet

WITH RYAN'S SAUCE

The most important thing about any dessert is not how it tastes, it's how it looks. This dessert isn't anything special, but it's five raspberries spread out on a plate, with a sauce drizzled over it, and doesn't that just seem like something that would be a dessert?

5 fresh-elected raspberries	1 Ryan

1. Gather literally thousands of raspberries from a raspberry tree or bush (we forget if raspberries come from a tree or bush [or from the grass]).

2. Hold a Raspberry Election, in which you and your wife and kids vote on which five raspberries are the best.

3. Distribute the five elected berries evenly onto one of those small round plates.

4. Call up Ryan and invite him over. Ask him to bring that delicious sauce he makes.

CONTINUED

5. When Ryan arrives, talk to him about how it's weird that you guys are seeing each other for the second time in a week (remember, you guys had Frautéed Bull Joints the other day and he brought over his Rice? Remember?). Anyway, ask him how things have been since the other day; show him your remodeled garage; tell him about the sushi documentary you watched last night.

6. Drizzle sauce over raspberries.

7. Tell Ryan to please leave.

TUCCI GORDO!!

"THE FOOD IN THE WOODS IS TERRIBLE."

—*Henry David Thoreau,*

PHILOSOPHER AND AUTHOR

Ultimate Gushy Protein Sewage Blast

WITH MIZRETTI INSANITY BOOST
(COCAINE)

Smoothies are a great way to feel healthy and be lazy at the same time. This is our favorite smoothie because it's green colored (so it has to be good for you). And because we keep a blender on our nightstand, we don't even have to get out of bed or open our eyes to make it.

- **1** banana (just the white stick part)
- **1** lumberjack's handful pokey berries
- **10** tree leaves
- **1** bale hay
- **½** cup peanut water

- **½** chunky cup curdled monkey's milk
- **½** cup salt nectar
- **1** smoothie-mix packet
- **4** frozen water chunks
- **1** ounce 100 percent pure, uncut cocaine (for the boost)

CONTINUED

1. Put ingredients into blender.

2. Blend dem 'gredients.

3. While blending, add in Mizretti Insanity Boost (cocaine).

NOTE: We prefer to use organic, single-sourced, shade-grown cocaine from the Antioquia region of Colombia. It helps to maintain our healthy lifestyle and to support our local cocaine dealer, D-Riggs.

---

4. Drink smoothie straight from the blender because, hey, why not? #yolo

STANLEY TUCCI!!

DID YOU KNOW: Bananas used to be illegal to consume because of their strong resemblance to a male dick.

Sweet Pork Smear

AND TIN WHISTLE CAKES

You don't always have to cook alone. Sometimes, cooking with a friend can be more fun and a lot easier. Especially if it's your old friend Ryan!

SERVES 1

1 hog's ass	¼ Irish pipe flaür
1 hog's mouth	1 bastard egg, dicked around
1 hog's dick	2 closed spoons dipped in
a pinch of road dust	sweet oil
1 tiny, doll-size bale of hay	1 Ryan

1. Call your friend Ryan and have him pick up the ingredients listed above.

2. Over the phone, tell Ryan to take the hog parts and smear each one on a clean white plate.

3. Drive to Ryan's house and, after breaking in, demand that he sprinkle the plate with road dust. Tell him to set it aside.

4. Force Ryan to break apart tiny bale of hay and combine with flaür.

CONTINUED

5. Make Ryan douse with dicked-around bastard egg. Then have him slowly drizzle sweet oil over mixture and combine.

6. Command him to stuff 10 handfuls of batter into a traditional tin whistle. Tell Ryan to then place on a cookie flat and shove into a towering inferno for 30 minutes.

7. When cake is finished, instruct him to remove from mold and place aside. Let Ryan know that he has to do this 5 more times because he's making a total of 6 cakes. 5 + 1 = 6. Duh.

8. Hold a gun to Ryan's head and tell him he has to arrange the cakes around your pork-smeared plate and drizzle with remaining sweet oil.

9. Tell Ryan to please leave.

PIZUTTI MILUTTI!!

"COME WITH ME, FOLLOWERS. THIS WAY. TO LUNCH."

—*Joseph Smith,* FOUNDER OF MORMONISM

HERE ARE SOME more of our delicious, original sweet concluders. We're not printing the recipes, though, because we just now realized that if we give them away, people can make them whenever they want for free, instead of coming to our restaurant and paying us to make them. We wouldn't get to be special anymore. Actually, now we feel bad for printing any recipes at all.

Salted Fat-n-Sugar Buckets

Artisanal Cubed Ice Draped with a Stevia Skin Rash

Coconut Cottage Curds Housed in a Crumbling Vanilla Tenement

Mentally Challenged Pineapple Parts

5-Foot-9 155-Pound Cake

Plain, Powdery Cookies

Tangy White Jiggle Mold Dying in a Coffee Sinkhole

Cocoa-Corroded Chicken Dunkers

Strawberry Cummed-on Tit Muffins

Hot Garbage Soufflé with Sweet Pickle Stripes

Cardamom Lullies Curled Up in a Papasan–Puff Pastry Chair

White-Men Spit-On Crustless Chess Pie

Cowpoke Haycakes with a Tobacco-Chew Topper

Cundy-Poached Meanies Staring up at You

Sand-Rolled Sticky Balls Pitched to Home Plate

Festered Custard with Bastard Mustard

Dessert Fish

Crumb Selection

Door-Slammed Strawberries with British Fart Tarts

Bananas Johnson

Footlong Frostingdogs

Blended-Up Cake Re-formed into Cake

Hot Melted Crayon Wax served in Discarded Monopoly Thimbles

Unsweetened Plastic Shards

DID YOU KNOW: Each food is associated with a memory. The memory for chocolate chips is World War I.

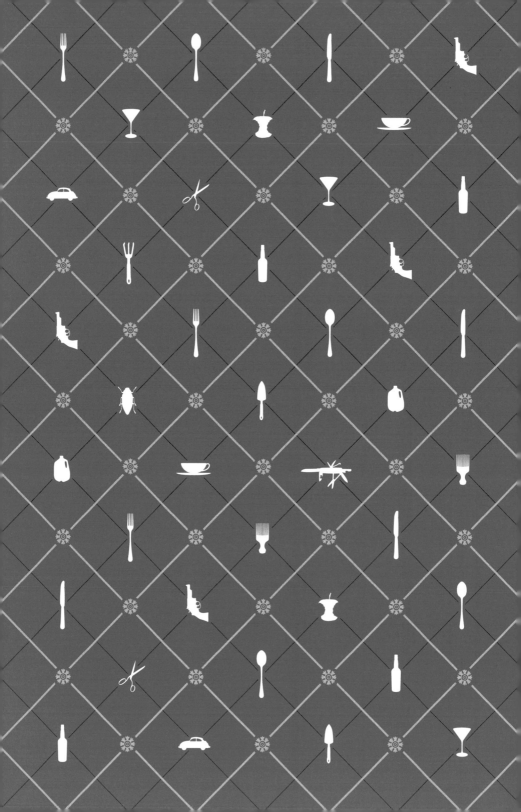

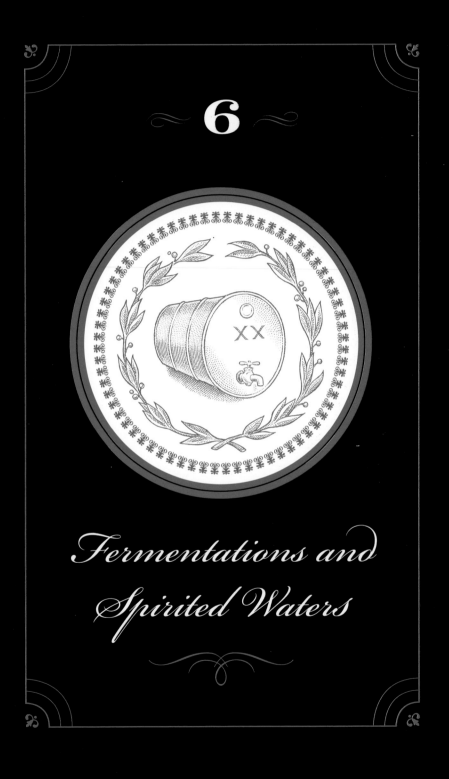

~6~

Fermentations and Spirited Waters

FERMENTATIONS and SPIRITED WATERS PRAYER

O spirits and ferments, pour thyself into me like a marvelous free-flowing fountain. Give me the spirit of a king, possess me like an ox and cheese and oh some olives and Triscuits would be really good right about now. Would it be weird if I just had some peanut butter right out of the jar? Ha ha ha penis butter. I'M HAVING A REALLY GOOD TIME RIGHT NOW. I AM DRONKK :). **AMEN.**

FERMENTATIONS

THROUGHOUT HISTORY, WINE (or, as we prefer to call it, "fermentations") has always been the beverage of choice for everyone from the ancient Greek gods to modern single female alcoholics. The following wines pair perfectly with nearly all of our recipes, not because of the flavors or textures or anything, but because if you drink enough, you'll be drunk and the food will taste really good.

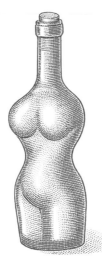

1996 BLONDE CORSAGE:

A buxom, curvaceous wine, popular to drink if you're crying in the bathroom. Pairs well with old Polaroids of your college boyfriend, Brandon.

1988 DODGE CARAVAN:

A rusty, bumpy wine. Good for getting drunk and driving a car.

1972 AMBROGINO:

Coarse and filthy, this grape is the basis of wines from the Monte Calvo region of Campania, Italy, a region known for its sodomy and knife violence.

2003 ARIDABIA:

A parched, desiccated, bone-dry red wine that's so dry that even the Sahara Desert was like, "Damn, that's some dry-ass wine."

2001 BIG-TIME CRABBY:

Apple wine made from nasty crab apples found on the ground in a cider mill. A nose tickle of hayrides, rotten pumpkins, and feet.

2013 BARREL WATER:

Combining the essences of tap water and the insides of old, dirty wine barrels, one will taste hints of hydrogen, oxygen, and old, dirty barrels.

1978 PINOT SUCK-O:

A white wine with a balanced taste, its tropical aromas and round, light feel make it ideal for sensitizing the palate before a meal, even though it's just a fucking bottle of wine.

1997 BREAKFAST WINE:

This refreshing, citrusy wine boasts a 25 percent ABV. Pairs well with Honey Nut Cheerios and brushing your teeth.

1995 SAUVIGNON LEBLANC:

A broad white wine made by star of the popular sitcom *Friends* Matt LeBlanc. Its goofy aroma and slapsticky flavor make it perfect for getting together with friends and ordering a pizza.

2008 ROUILLOUIILOUILLIOUILLION:

Sometimes it's hard to describe what a wine tastes like. It's good, though. You'll like it. Whatever.

1997 VINTAGE PORT:

This putrid dessert port was accidentally aged three years in a casket, instead of a cask. When they asked us to age the port, we thought they said "casket," and we were so confused. We were like, "Why would they ask us to age it in a casket? Aren't dead people put in a casket?" But we weren't sure if we'd get in trouble for asking, so we just went ahead and aged it in a casket. So, yeah. It was aged in a casket.

2016 MONSTER ENERGY WINE:

Hints of taurine and inositol deliver the big bad buzz that only Monster Energy Wine can give you. Tear into a bottle of one of the meanest energy wine brews you'll find!!!

1973 BROADWAY WINE:

This overpriced, mediocre wine is served during intermissions at Broadway musicals. Great for loosening up the audience member who is annoyed with Nathan Lane's performance.

2010 GREG SHAPIRO PRIVATE SELECTION MALBEC:

Made by local winemaker Greg Shapiro, this blend of traditional Bordeaux varietals tastes exactly like Greg Shapiro. You'd have to know Greg Shapiro to understand, but still, it's weird and impressive.

2006 KINDERGARTEN KIDS WINE:

A playful white wine with shy flavors and a sticky after-mouth. Perfect for kids. They hate the taste of it, but once they drink enough, they start acting really funny.

1999 RAINBOW LIFE RIESLING:

This riesling is a blend of everything in the world. It displays a spicy acidity balanced with notes of rocks and sand and tacos and bananas and crickets and dust and earwax and lily pads and grapefruit and hockey pucks and paper and brick and aged cheddar and old film strips and cake and armor and textbooks and factories and social injustice and cigars and skin and hair and TV and leather jackets and paper and floppy disks and femininity and burlap.

1988 TREVOR MARX WINE:

This little shit of a red wine will try to kiss you with a skinny, weak tongue and will undo your bra with shaky, wet fingers. Notes of sweat, underwear, and white bread.

2001 A SPACE ODYSSEY:

Not a wine, but an incredible movie.

"FOOD IS LIKE COMEDY."

—Judd Apatow,

COMEDIAN AND FILM DIRECTOR

SPIRITED WATERS

COCKTAILS (or, as we prefer to call them, "spirited waters") after dinner are a great way to finish a meal. And a cocktail *with* dinner—now, that's even better. Cocktails add so much to brunch, lunch, and even breakfast every day. We like to have cocktails with everything we do. In fact, you might say we can't function without them. Try some of these original Mizretti cocktails as often as you can!

WEIRD OLD MR. GRANDPEAR

2 ounces Mizretti family
  rubbing alcohol
1 ounce pear schnapps

1 ounce Mizretti brand sambuca
1 ounce canned pear slices
2 ounces old coffee grounds

* Shake rubbing alcohol, schnapps, and sambuca and strain into a dirty cocktail glass. Fondle the canned pear slices while staring at a younger woman, then plop them into the drink while laughing in a low, unsettling tone. Garnish with coffee grounds for horrible texture. Serve in a musty basement with lots of wood paneling.

LOUD RACIST

1 ounce vodka
1 ounce rum
1 ounce tequila

1 ounce moonshine
1 ounce absinthe

* Dump all clear-colored liquids into a tall glass with ice. Drink in one horrible gulp. Start yelling.

SEX WITH EVERYONE EVERYWHERE ALL THE TIME

2 ounces vodka
2 ounces peach schnapps
1 ounce coconut rum
1 ounce banana liqueur

1 ounce grapefruit juice
1 ounce lime juice
1 ounce grenadine syrup

CONTINUED

* Slosh all the liquids around together until you start to feel a little sick. Think about your life choices that have led you to this. Shed a tear. Serve.

THE MUSTACHE AND HAT

1 ounce Old Southern Bearded
Man rye whiskey

1 ounce Pimm's

1 ounce Dr. Mizretti's house
ginger bitters

½ teaspoon raw organic honey

1 orange peel

1 basil plant

* Combine the whiskey, Pimm's, and bitters with 2 to 3 artisanal ice cubes in a mixing glass. Stir with stick made of locally sourced oakwood. Strain the whiskey mixture into a Ball mason jar. Massage honey onto rim of jar for a long enough time to make it seem like you're important. Dangle the orange peel over the jar but don't drop it in. Just dangle. Garnish drink with an entire potted basil plant. Serve to person with annoying facial hair.

> "WE'RE GONNA NEED A BIGGER SODA."
>
> —*Martin Brody*, JAWS

MEG'S PANTIES

4 ounces spiced rum

1 ounce Jimmy's Ripe Peach
Schnapps

juice from ½ a lemon

½ ounce heavy whipping cream
floater

* In a shaker, combine rum, schnapps, lemon juice, and a scoop of ice. Shake relentlessly until your hand is sore. Pour contents into a cooler glass and top off with whipping cream floater. Sip and think of the first time you fingered a girl.

HOT HORSE PISS

1 slice lemon

1 ounce apple cider vinegar

2 ounces water

1 ounce wheatgrass

1 dash turmeric

1½ ounces whiskey

1 bag yerba mate	1 stick asparagus

* Combine the lemon, vinegar, and water in a small pot and heat until boiling. As water begins rolling, add in wheatgrass and turmeric to give it a nice, stinky earthiness. Top off with whiskey. Pour pungent drink into mug and steep yerba mate bag for an even more pee-like stink. Garnish with asparagus stick for the ultimate horse piss drink.

KENTUCKY DESK DRAWER

2 dashes root beer	1 smushed-up orange wedge
2½ ounces Kentucky bourbon	1 pinch chewing tobacco
1 dash Original Pine-Sol disinfectant cleaner	

* A drink for a real man in a big hat. Combine the root beer, bourbon whiskey, and Pine-Sol with 2 to 3 ice cubes in a mixing glass. Stir with power drill until the ice has been crushed and destroyed. Mangle orange wedge by stomping it and beating it up. Then place it at the bottom of a rocks glass. Pour drink mixture over it while coughing hard. Garnish with a wad of chaw.

PATHETIC TERRORIST BUS BOMB

¾ pint foreign beer	1 lit match
½ shot 100 proof rum	1 scoop mint chocolate chip ice cream
½ shot moonshine	

* Pour beer into pint glass. Drop shot glasses of rum and moonshine into beer. To consume, scream at the top of your lungs and chug all of it at once. Then light match and throw it down your throat. Chase with a scoop of ice cream to apologize to your body. Then apologize to everyone in bar. Leave with head down.

"FOOD IS GOOD / I LIKE FOOD / SORRY, I'M TOO HUNGRY TO THINK OF A RHYME RIGHT NOW."

—*Dr. Seuss*, AUTHOR

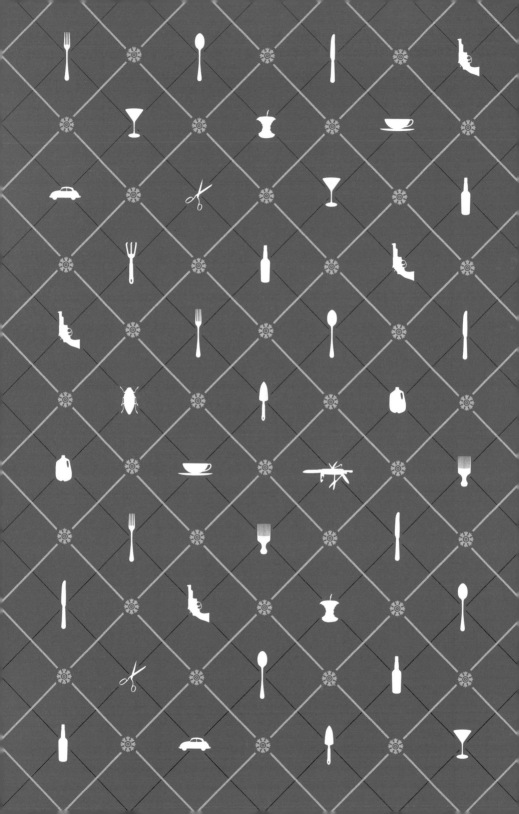

7

Brunchments

A

RE YOU A BAD PERSON? THEN WE

know you love eating brunch! Because you

bought the book, you get an exclusive sneak

peek of our brunch menu. Please do not show this to anyone who

has not purchased the book. Make them show you the receipt.

BAGELS
Stacked on a dildo, smeared with cream cheese along the sides

11

EGGS GLORBY
Scrumpled with tamaters

10

EGG BUB-BLÉ
*Demolished by shrapneled potatoes and oozing
with oil-cream rebar*

14

WILD DOG FRED'S HUNGRY BOY SKILLET

15

HUEVOS MACHISMOS

12

LA OMELETTE
*Flattened bright-and-yellow eggies suspended in a smog cloud
of polluted cheese*

16

BILL CLINTON BREAKFAST SANDWICH

15

SWEATY COW NUBS
Sunbathing on an egg-white towel

10

Chubby Meat Panels

Tied up in a biscuit patch and waterboarded with boiling cream

12

PankPanks

Stuffed with three-stick compote (tree, twig, big)

13

Apple-Onion PankPanks

Made by mistake, served with a note of apology

12

Fluffed Oak Leaves

Spackled with crab cheese and a Vinny Gret™ drenching

11

Raisin-Only Salad

Served under a whole watermelon

9

Oatmeal

*Dumped from a paper packet into a little bowl
of microwaved water*

8

A Styrofoam Cup with Two Grapes in It

9

Cornflakes and Lettuce Leaves

14

Breakfast Beef Stroganoff

With Breakfast Baked Potato and Breakfast Steamed Vegetables.
Served with Breakfast Soup or Breakfast Caesar Salad

19

NEXT TOS

Dinkies-n-linkies	5
Cloat Bacon	7
Scripted Words	6
P-Seed 20s	5
Pig Cleavage	6
Flicked Peanut Butter Glob	3
Levitating Wheat Puffs	4
Really Cold Peanuts	2
Apartment Potato	5

TONGUE SIPPERS

Housemade Chunky Marnie	11
Moesha Sparkling Drink Beverage Liquid	10

Siphoned Fruit Milk Served with an Entire Bottle of Whiskey and a Tiny Umbrella 12

Brown Foam 13

Wrigley's Spearmint Gum Bourbon 12

Wrung-Out Dish-Towel Water (hot or cold) 10

PERFECTION-STYLE COFFEES

South Pacific Double D Tit-Roast Served in Monkey Prong Press 3.5

Hazelbeak Donka Dong Coffee (Regular or Horrible) . . 4

Coffee with Food in the Bottom 8

DID YOU KNOW: No buffet line has ever turned into a conga line.

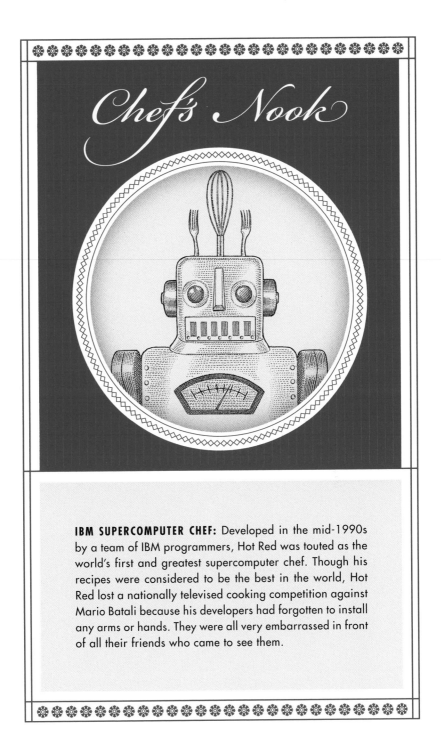

Chef's Nook

IBM SUPERCOMPUTER CHEF: Developed in the mid-1990s by a team of IBM programmers, Hot Red was touted as the world's first and greatest supercomputer chef. Though his recipes were considered to be the best in the world, Hot Red lost a nationally televised cooking competition against Mario Batali because his developers had forgotten to install any arms or hands. They were all very embarrassed in front of all their friends who came to see them.

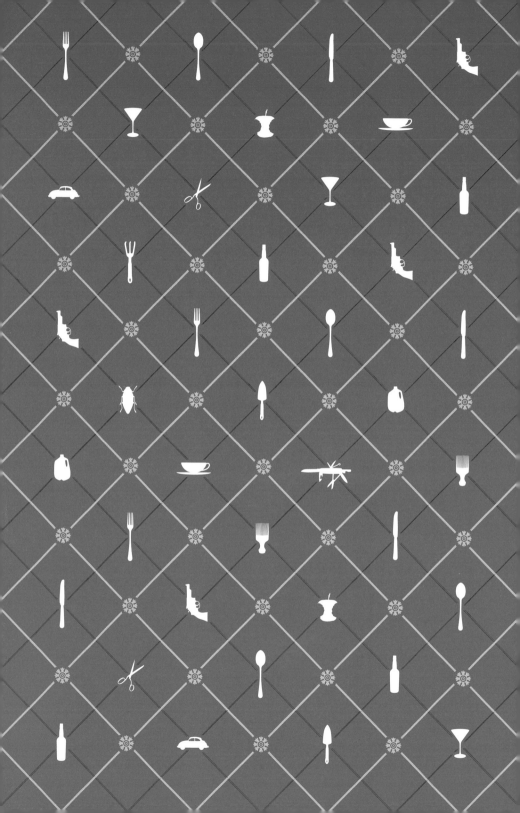

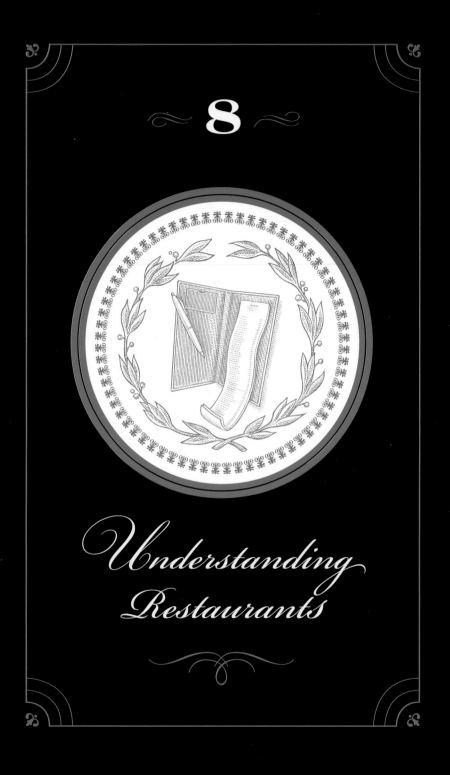

8

Understanding
Restaurants

THE FUDS DINING EXPERIENCE IS *the best dining experience you can get. But sometimes, FUDS gets so crowded that we ask customers to eat standing up or in the bathroom. When FUDS gets too crowded, people have to go to a different restaurant. This is why we want to tell you about restaurants in general.*

The main drawback of restaurants is that you must pay for the food you eat, as opposed to cooking for yourself, in which you pay the grocery store cashier but by the time you're eating you've forgotten that you paid for the meal.

Whereas most people who cook for themselves are unmarried and reclusive, most people who eat at restaurants do so with friends, family, and people they're hooking up with.

WHO'S IN A RESTAURANT?

I **T TAKES MORE** than two thousand people to operate a single restaurant. Some restaurants are even considered their own cities (Akron, Ohio).

When you enter a restaurant, you will see many different people. Don't worry, these people aren't going to hurt you or start calling you names like "little bitch" or "turkey head." Rather, these people work in a restaurant, so they belong there. If you plan on eating at a restaurant, it is important that you understand who each person is and what he does.

COOK

The cook works in the kitchen of the restaurant, using ingredients to prepare meals. He is considered the luckiest member of the restaurant's staff because he works with food all the time, so he can eat food whenever he wants. A cook is given items like wooden spoons and turkey basters, which allow him to easily eat food and drink sauces while cooking.

WAITER

The waiter is the person who walks up to you while you are sitting down and asks you what you want to eat and drink. Unlike the cook, the waiter has a hard time eating food on the job. Much of the waiter's job consists of bringing you food and taking away your plate when you're done. It's sort of degrading. This is why waiters often complain about their lives.

NOTE: A female waiter is called a **womanwaiter**.

HOSTESS

The hostess is a sexy young woman dressed in black pants and a tight black shirt that sometimes shows a little bit of cleavage. Her job is to take reservations and to show you to your seat, so there's not much food involved. If the hostess gets hungry, she can eat a bunch of peppermints from the bowl up front, or she can steal rolls from the back and eat them out of her pockets when no one's looking.

LIVE BAND

The live band plays rock and roll music from the back of the restaurant to keep the atmosphere upbeat. The live band consists of a guitarist, a bassist, a guy on keyboards, a drummer, and a lead singer. Two of them are brothers. They fight about who gets to sing which songs, and their music sucks.

FOOD ENHANCER

A well-groomed, well-dressed man, usually about the age of sixty, who crouches under the table once customers have received their meals. As they eat their food, the food enhancer breathes deeply, rubs the customer's lap, and whispers things like, "Mmmm, baby likey? Yeah, you're a bad little boy. You want more, hmm?"

BATHROOM LADY

A lady named Barbara who shows you where the bathroom is.

BATHROOM TROLL

A hideous creature who lurks in the bathroom stall and hides inside the toilet when you have to use it. He is the one who replaces the toilet paper every night. He makes $5.75 an hour.

BARTENDER

Bartenders are like cooks who make concoctions out of alcohol. The bartender gets to eat all the alcohol he wants while he's working. This is why bartenders are grouchy and always die at an early age.

FOOD REF

The food ref makes sure everything at the restaurant is fair so that your meal runs smoothly. If you break a rule, he will penalize you.

BUSBOY

The busboy is the person who sets tables, cleans tables, and takes dirty dishes to the dishwasher. The busboy is, in fact, always a boy, never a man. Right now you're probably thinking that you've seen busboys who are men. Nope, you're wrong. They were all boys. Little eight-year-old boys.

MANAGER

The manager is in charge of the restaurant and he is always a huge fucking asshole. He makes sure the restaurant is running efficiently and he has a goatee and he fucking sucks. He's in his early forties and he's twenty pounds overweight and when he has sex he comes immediately.

FOOD PENALTIES

Burping: Two minutes in the coatroom

Too many crumbs on the tablecloth: Four minutes in the coatroom

Sharing: Five minutes in the coatroom

Excessive slurping: Six minutes in the coatroom and single-meal suspension

Trying the "pull-the-tablecloth-under-the-table-setting" trick: Seven minutes in the coatroom

Third-degree murder: Life in the coatroom

DID YOU KNOW: Before he founded McDonald's, Ronald McDonald had a brief stint as a backup infielder for the Washington Senators.

INTERVIEW WITH
JENKY LOGAN

LEADING THE ARTISANAL BUSBOY
REVOLUTION

WHEN WE HIRED our head busboy, we wanted someone who would bring as much pride to dumping food into the trash as we do to dumping food into people's mouths. Someone who was cool and young and hip and wore suspenders. And we found what we were looking for in Jenky Logan, the ultimate artisan busboy.

JENKY, COULD YOU EXPLAIN YOUR BUSING METHOD?

I developed an entirely new approach by returning to our busboy roots. Today, with the Internet and smartphones, we've lost sight of what it means to truly bus a table. I just wanted to go back to the way things were. Everything used to always be better.

AND HOW EXACTLY ARE YOU APPROACHING IT?

I looked at my grandfather's diaries, which were very embarrassing for him. He did a lot of weird things. But he also wrote about what it was like to be a busboy in the forties and fifties, before everything became so digitized. He did it all with his hands. After reading his diary, I wanted to follow suit. Now I only use the most natural bleach water and organic cotton rags. All the animal products I bus with are hormone-free and sourced from local farms. We don't actually use any animal products, though.

WHAT BROUGHT YOU TO BUSING?

Busing is as important, if not more important, than the meal itself. Without cleaning, how could you have a clean table to eat on again?

WE DISAGREE WITH THAT. THE COOKING IS MUCH
MORE IMPORTANT.

Okay. Whatever.

WELL, THIS INTERVIEW IS OVER A PAGE LONG, SO WE
HAVE TO STOP, BUT THANK YOU FOR BEING IN OUR
BOOK. WE'LL PAY YOU AFTER IT'S RELEASED.

Oh, do you know when it's going to be released?

WE'RE NOT SURE YET. WE'RE STILL TALKING WITH THE
PUBLISHERS. WE'RE HOPING SOMETIME MID–NEXT
YEAR, BUT, YOU KNOW, WHO KNOWS? HEY, SO, AFTER
WE CLOSE, WE WERE THINKIN' OF HITTING UP A FEW
BARS AROUND TOWN. ANY INTEREST?

Um, I think I might have like a friend in town, and she's gonna call
me to meet up, so I don't think I can.

ALL RIGHT, COOL, WELL, SHE'S WELCOME, TOO. IF
YOU CHANGE YOUR MIND JUST LET US KNOW. DID
YOU DROP THAT PEN?

No, I think that's your pen.

OKAY, THANKS.

Okay . . .

SHORTHAND

THINGS MOVE PRETTY quickly at restaurants. In fact, things move so quickly sometimes that we don't even know if they really happened. One night, after working an eight-hour shift, Alfredo said that he didn't remember anything (brain aneurysm?). But if you want to serve people swiftly and efficiently, you've got to have a shorthand system. Here is ours.

86

Currently out of a specific item
EXAMPLE: *"86 the corn bread. We lost it all."*

15

Too many onions. Someone must go back to the kitchen to eat some onions.
EXAMPLE: *"15! 15! Get back in the kitchen. It's a 15—you know, the onion-code thing. You gotta eat some."*

11

11 of something
EXAMPLE: *"We have 11 side dishes."*

CR

Cooked ruined
EXAMPLE: *"How would you like your cheeseburger?" "CR, please."*

CCR

If the surviving members of Creedence Clearwater Revival are eating at your table.
EXAMPLE: *"The still-alive members of CCR would each like a glass of clear water."*

EOTS

Everything on the side

EXAMPLE: *"I'll have a Cobb Salad, EOTS."*

3F

Form the food into a face

EXAMPLE: *"I'll have scrambled eggs and sausage, and can you 3F?"*

CTBP

Cut into baby pieces so I can feel like I'm a baby

EXAMPLE: *"I'll have the hot dog CTBP."*

VMTR

Chicken

EXAMPLE: *"I'll have the chicken." "VMTR?" "Uhhh...what?"*

SAND

Sandwich

EXAMPLE: *"I'd like to order one plate, SAND."*

NO-SAND

No sandwich

EXAMPLE: *"I would like the lasagna, NO-SAND."*

"MAN SHALL NOT LIVE ON CHIPS AND SALSA ALONE. THOSE
ARE FOR WHEN YOU'RE WAITING FOR YOUR MEXICAN FOOD."

—Matthew 4:4

THE MIZRETTI MANEUVER

IT IS A WELL-KNOWN FACT THAT YOU or someone you are dining with will most likely choke at some point during your visit to a restaurant. The social pressures and extreme intensity of eating in a restaurant often cause the eater's windpipe to constrict and tighten, resulting in blockage by a piece of food. At FUDS, we take a more organic approach to preventing suffocation and encourage you to use our method in other restaurants as well. Follow these simple steps.

1.

The choking victim will signal for help by lightly scratching his chin. He will look like he is thinking about something. NOTE: He will scratch his chin again to cancel the signal.

2.

Use one hand to grab victim's hair, and with your free hand, clasp together victim's ankles.

3.

Lift victim and rotate his body 90 degrees so that he is parallel to the carpet.

4.

Compress victim like accordion over and over until he begins giggling.

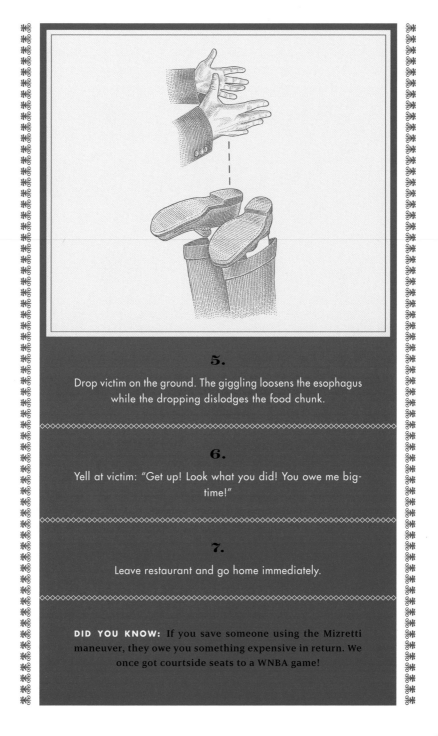

5.

Drop victim on the ground. The giggling loosens the esophagus while the dropping dislodges the food chunk.

6.

Yell at victim: "Get up! Look what you did! You owe me big-time!"

7.

Leave restaurant and go home immediately.

DID YOU KNOW: If you save someone using the Mizretti maneuver, they owe you something expensive in return. We once got courtside seats to a WNBA game!

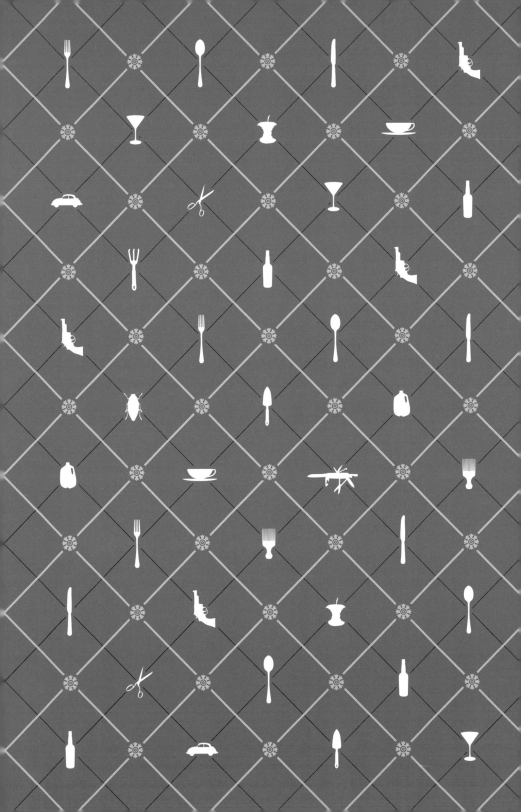

9

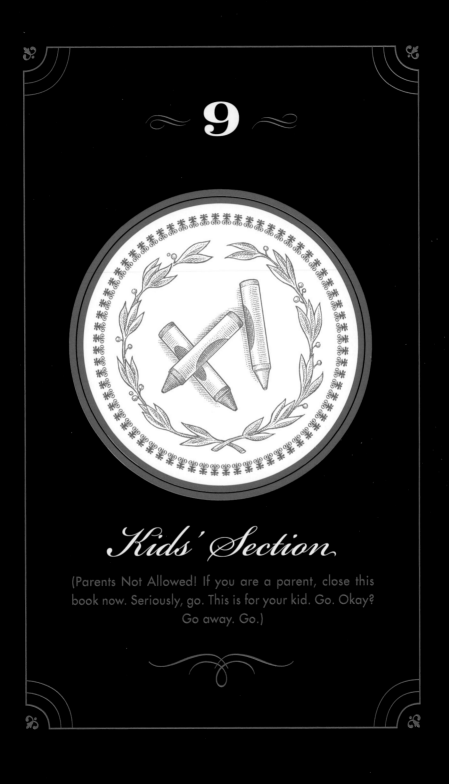

Kids' Section

(Parents Not Allowed! If you are a parent, close this
book now. Seriously, go. This is for your kid. Go. Okay?
Go away. Go.)

H
EY KID! WE KNOW YOU DON'T
have the thought capacity to sit down and
actually comprehend writing, so here's a
silly activity section just for YOU! Draw, color, cut, glue, and
generally act like the senseless, unfinished version of a person
that you really are! WHEEEEEE!!!

LET'S COLOR!

White bread

Paper plate

White socks

White American cheese

White underwear

Glass of milk

Snowy ground

Chef's hat
(white)

UNSCRAMBLE THE FOODS!

Hey kid! Unscramble the words of these yummy foreign delicacies!

(See answers at bottom of page.)

MEXICO: licseh ne daagon

FRANCE: ragstapeeedoif

RUSSIA: йобаскоо и йотпасу

JAPAN: 口身グマ

BRAILLE: ⠄⠶⠲⠶⠆ ⠦⠲⠲

CHEF'S HATS FROM AROUND THE WORLD

Hey kid! You've probably seen an American chef's hat before, right? It's a tall white hat with a full pouched crown. But did you know that chef's hats are different all around the world? Check it out, kid!

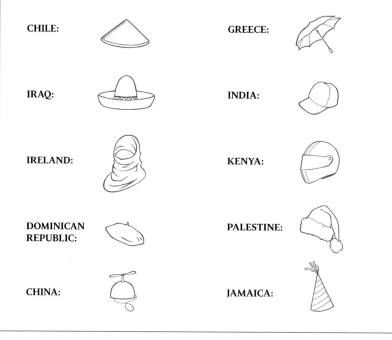

CHILE:

IRAQ:

IRELAND:

DOMINICAN REPUBLIC:

CHINA:

GREECE:

INDIA:

KENYA:

PALESTINE:

JAMAICA:

MEXICO: chiles en nogada • FRANCE: pâté de foie gras • RUSSIA: колбасой и капустой • JAPAN: マグロ身口 • BRAILLE: ⠦⠲⠲ ⠄⠶⠲⠶⠆

TWO OF A KIND

Hey kid! Draw a line to pair your favorite food and wine!

Chicken Nuggets	**Sauvignon Blanc**
Grilled Cheese	**Pinot Grigio**
Plain Hamburger	**Red Zinfandel**
French Fries	**Pinot Noir**
Chocolate Cupcake	**Brachette D'Acqui**

A-MAZE-IN SMALL INTESTINE

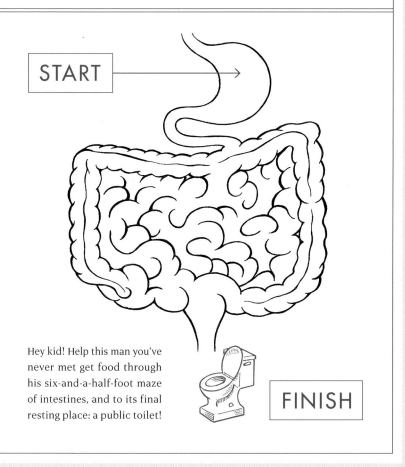

Hey kid! Help this man you've never met get food through his six-and-a-half-foot maze of intestines, and to its final resting place: a public toilet!

FINISH

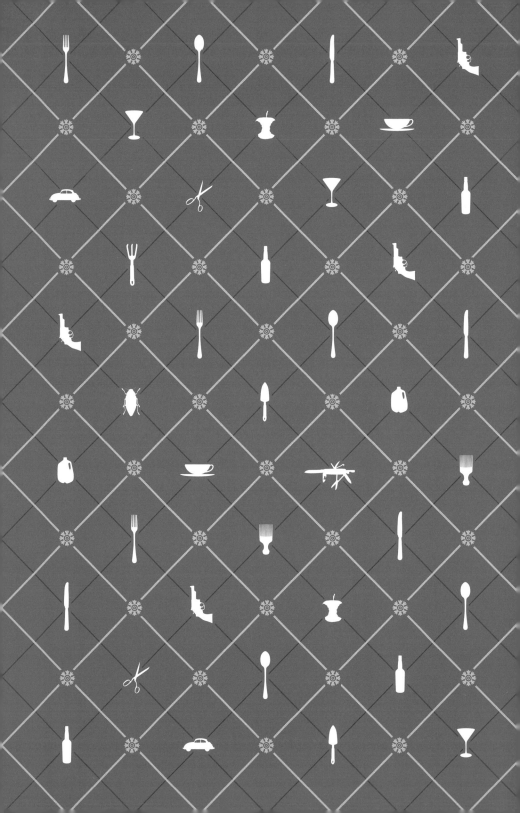

~ **10** ~

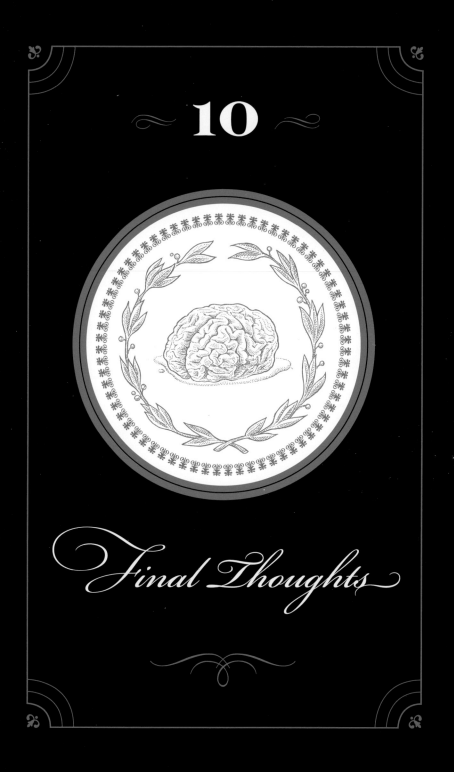

Final Thoughts

**E LIVE IN A TIME OF PERVA-** *sive global unrest. With climate change, economic recessions, and international tensions reaching a boiling point, we must ask ourselves: What does this mean for the current state of food?*

Nothing. It means nothing about food. I mean, have you had any food lately? It's delicious. It's so good. In conclusion, food is so good. Go eat some food.

HOW TO COOK THIS BOOK

CONGRATULATIONS! YOU'VE FINISHED reading the *FUDS Complete Encyclofoodia*. Now you know how to cook a dead dog, save a pathetic choking victim, and make baby carrots (carrot sex). That means it's time to properly dispose of this book. Don't worry, our book is made up of 100 percent organic artisanal ingredients, so not only is it edible, but it's also biodegradable—so when you defecate its remains into the dirt, a tree will grow. Thanks for reading and *Bono tito!*

Signed,
The Mizretti Brothers

To cook this book, you'll need:

1 *FUDS Complete Encyclofoodia*	**2 cups Original Flavor™** water
14 dry tree twigs	**1 packet book spices**
2 flint rocks	

1. Dig hole in ground and pile dry sticks inside.

2. Standing over the stick pile, scratch flint rocks together quickly and harshly enough to start fire. Feel free to mutter curse words during this step, as it is difficult and you will probably hurt one or two of your fingers.

3. Admire the burning glory that is fire. It is beautiful. It is life. It is death. It is all of us.

4. Put Original Flavor™ water in pot over the fire to boil.

5. Place book in pot. Make sure water level is high enough that it overflows and spills all over the place.

6. After book has softened significantly, remove it with bare hands so it hurts a lot.

7. Open packet of book spices and effeminately shake book spices over soaking-wet book.

Now your book is cool and ready to be consumed. Thanks for reading the *FUDS Complete Encyclofoodia*, and please remember to enjoy these other titles from Bloomsbury:

How to Cook a Duck: Could Someone Please Explain It to Us?

1,001 Dirty Jokes about Dirty Kitchens

Wrongald McDongald: Deception and Lies from a Fast Food Oligarchy

What the Heck's a Bread Bowl? by Paul Reiser

We Never Use the Dining Room: A Novel

Cobbler's Cobbler: Shoes and Fruits

In Defense of Place Mats

Photos of Fruit Arranged Like a Penis and Balls

Food Dudes: The Cultural Impact of the Eating Habits of Jimi Hendrix, Bob Dylan, and Jim Morrison

The Vegetarian's Guide to Eating out of the Trash

"Food isn't just food. Food is more than food." —US

BOOK DESSERT

THIS BOOK COULD not have been written or published without the assistance of Jillian Weiss-Edelstein of the Silver Napkin Board, J. Osterios of Western Kitchens, Ryan, and of course, Jessica Hess. For historical facts and information, we have to thank the Shipkiss Table & Tablecloth Foundation.

THANK YOU, Mr. and Mrs. Danky, for your generous donation toward the book. You are total strangers to us otherwise. And we didn't ask for any donations.

THANK YOU TO the following organizations, companies, charities, and funds: Congregation Beth Israel, the Walk Against Pregnancy, the French Toast Squad, the Knife Group, Larry Groaten's Bread, Zip Cola, the Armadillo and Leather Museum, Phyllis's Bagels and Specialty Beverages, the Intelligence Sub-Committee on Interstate Transit Legislation, and Gary and Tracy's Penis Design.

WE WOULD LIKE to make a special mention of Hornet Gravy Distributors, Ben Teacher and Allisyn Grissom-Nostrus, Paddles Sex Club, Burt Sixty-Four, Nathan Garbage-Trash, Guy Forrest of KitchenWhisk Media, Eleanor Wheezing-Coughing, Cindy Teff of grapesandapples.com, Gary Shrunt, Gayne Pinn, and, of course, none of this would have been possible without the generosity and support of Jessica Hess.

TO OUR ENTIRE staff at FUDS, who kept the restaurant running while we stayed home in our big bed working on this book, you all deserve special recognition for your hard work. You will not be getting that, though, because that wouldn't be fair to everyone else. Also, please stop reading this and get back to work.

THANK YOU TO Richard Stick at HealthCo. Fruit Preserves for all his advice, suggestions, and charts—none of which we used. And of course thank you to Jessica Hess for embracing our vision, feeling compassion, and driving the project through the complicated production phase into its final form.

THANK YOU Kelly Hudson, Dan Klein, and Arthur Meyer for actually writing this book, because we're not real and you made us up. In fact, one of you is typing this right now (Dan). Thank you.

AND, OF COURSE, thank you, Jessica Hess.